The Science of Sports

The Editors of *Scientific American*

SCIENTIFIC AMERICAN EDUCATIONAL PUBLISHING

New York

Published in 2023 by Scientific American Educational Publishing
in association with **The Rosen Publishing Group**
29 East 21st Street, New York, NY 10010

Contains material from Scientific American®, a division of Springer Nature America, Inc.,
reprinted by permission, as well as original material from The Rosen Publishing Group®.

First Edition

Scientific American
Lisa Pallatroni: Project Editor

Rosen Publishing
Joseph Kampff: Compiling Editor
Michael Moy: Senior Graphic Designer

Cataloging-in-Publication Data
Names: Scientific American, inc.
Title: The science of sports / edited by the Editors of Scientific American.
Description: New York : Scientific American Educational Publishing, 2023. |
Series: Scientific American explores big ideas | Includes glossary and index.
Identifiers: ISBN 9781684169214 (pbk.) | ISBN 9781684169221
(library bound) | ISBN 9781684169238 (ebook)
Subjects: LCSH: Sports sciences–Juvenile literature. |
Sports–Technological innovations–Juvenile literature.
Classification: LCC GV558.S354 2023 | DDC 796–dc23

Manufactured in the United States of America
Websites listed were live at the time of publication.

Cover: Master1305/Shutterstock.com

CPSIA Compliance Information: Batch # SACS23. For Further Information contact
Rosen Publishing, New York, New York at 1-800-237-9932.

CONTENTS

Section 3: Sports Technology

Section 4: Sports Culture

INTRODUCTION

S ports are a human universal: humans in all cultures play them, and they've done so for a long, long time. Human beings spend an enormous amount of time and money playing, watching, and thinking about sports. This book is for readers whose interest in sports and athleticism goes deeper than the stats of their favorite players and the standings of their favorite teams. The *Scientific American* articles collected here use science to answer questions about sports, such as: What makes some people so much better at sports than everyone else? How do the material properties of a ball affect the way it travels through the air? Is it possible to predict with reasonable certainty which team will win? Should transgender women be allowed to play in women's sports?

Section 1, "Athletic Bodies," looks at athleticism through a biological lens to determine what makes elite athletes so good. Section 2, "The Psychology of Sports," examines the psychology of sports, investigating, for example, the psychological effects of overtraining, the ways coaching strategies affect athletes, and the myth of hot hands in basketball. Section 3, "Sports Technology," looks at the effects of technology in sports, from the air pressure in a football and the composition of baseballs to the creation of high-tech prostheses for athletes with disabilities. The final section, "Sports Culture," takes a broader approach to sports. It looks at the ways sports interact with the larger culture. It investigates, for example, the problem of sports doping, the psychology behind taking a knee, and the effects of American slavery on professional football.

Section 1: Athletic Bodies

The Making of an Olympian

By Rachel Nuwer

Every Summer Olympics features a handful of superhumans the likes of Usain Bolt, Gabby Douglas and Michael Phelps. Rio will be no exception. With shows of supreme physical strength and grace, the standouts in the 2016 Games will sprint, flip and glide their way through a gauntlet of grueling events. They will captivate the crowds, smash records and, in all likelihood, leave Brazil with an impressive haul of gold.

But what, exactly, sets these superelite athletes apart? It has long been a matter of heated debate. Historically, experts and sports fans alike have believed that genes are primarily responsible for such extraordinary achievement: top athletes are simply born with superior physical traits that allow them to outperform everyone else. During the past three Summer Games, for instance, many analysts credited Phelps's stunning success in the pool—winning him a total of 22 medals—to his 80-inch "wingspan" and hyperflexible, flipperlike size-14 feet.

Since the 1990s, though, another school of thought has gained considerable traction—namely, the idea that inborn talent is not, in and of itself, enough to reach the highest echelons in sport. No matter how good someone is by nature, genuine expertise also demands certain psychological traits, as well as years of hard work and first-rate coaching. Sports psychologists are finding, for instance, that the experience of overcoming major emotional challenges can sometimes instill extra resilience in young athletes and fuel their exceptional drive. Genes, meanwhile, make a difference in how much individuals respond to training in addition to shaping their baseline gifts.

"For a long time people believed either you had innate talent or you didn't," says K. Anders Ericsson, a psychologist at Florida State University who coined the term "deliberate practice" for a training approach that involves goal setting, repetitions of component skills, mental rehearsals and immediate feedback—now seen as critical for elite athletes. His work, described in a new book, *Peak: Secrets from the New Science of Expertise*, debunks the idea of "naturals" who seem to come out of nowhere but have often just switched sports. "I've always found plausible alternative accounts that involve prior purposeful practice," Ericsson says.

In truth, going for gold probably always takes huge amounts of genetically bestowed potential, mental toughness and first-class training—as well as lots of luck to avoid injury, to connect with the right coach, and to find the best resources and support.

Fast, Faster, Fastest

Jerry Baltes, head cross-country and track coach at Grand Valley State University, often tells new recruits, "I can make you faster, but I can't make you fast." In fact, even among the already fast, so-called trainability varies. Levels of intrinsic fitness and achieved fitness—or what you can attain through training—are evaluated based on traits such as muscle strength and cardiorespiratory fitness, itself normally measured by the volume of oxygen the body consumes in a minute. Both can differ dramatically from one person to the next. For instance, a young Olympian may have three times the maximum oxygen uptake as an elderly person in poor health—and twice that of an unfit person the athlete's same age.

For some, achieved levels of fitness are hard to shift, no matter how much drive they have—in which case, pushing too hard can lead to overtraining instead of improvement. When exercise scientist Nir Eynon of the Institute of Sport, Exercise and Active Living (ISEAL) at Victoria University in Australia and his colleagues subjected sedentary people to the same carefully controlled exercise programs, they found that some made almost no gains; at the same time, others increased their cardiorespiratory fitness by as much as 50 to 80 percent. "If you take two people—you and me—and we start at the same baseline and do exactly the same training and eat the same diet, we would both gain aerobic capacity, or muscle mass—or whatever—very differently," Eynon says.

Elite athletes most likely are among a subset of people who reap the greatest benefits from training on top of high baseline levels of fitness. In 1998 geneticist Claude Bouchard of Pennington Biomedical Research Center of the Louisiana State University System and his colleagues found that both intrinsic and achieved levels of fitness tend to aggregate in families. When they tested 99 families, heritability explained about 50 percent of the variance in maximum oxygen uptake, for example. But Bouchard found no correlation between inborn fitness and trainability.

Of course, it all starts with the inborn gifts—as one 2014 study underscored. Evolutionary biologist Michael Lombardo of Grand Valley State University and his colleagues surveyed 15 male and female Olympic sprinting champions and the 20 fastest American men in U.S. history and found that, among those for whom biographical data were available, all were exceptionally fast before undergoing any formal training. Likewise, 64 collegiate championship-level sprinters and throwers in the same study all recalled being faster or stronger and better at throwing, respectively, than their peers as children. Of significance, the elite sprinters also showed big jumps in ability once they began formal training. "Strength, agility, speed and other athletic traits are all phenotypes that arise from interactions of the genotype with the environment," Lombardo says. "To deny that there is any genetic variation in individuals that results in differences in athletic ability is really denying what we know about biology."

That said, those underlying genetics have proved elusive. In 2016 Bouchard and his colleagues compared common alleles—or variants of a given gene—in 1,520 elite endurance athletes with 2,760 matched control subjects from four continents and came up completely empty-handed. "We thought we were in good shape to identify alleles, but it turns out that wasn't true at all," he says; the team "failed miserably," uncovering "not even one single allele reaching statistical significance." The takeaway? Athletic ability probably arises from multiple gene variants, all with very small effect sizes. One such variant, though, may be *ACTN3*—a gene responsible for producing a protein used by fast-twitch muscle fibers, which contract quickly and provide bursts of power.

In work that spanned more than a decade, geneticist Kathryn North of the University of Melbourne in Australia and her colleagues found that mice with *ACTN3* have greater endurance. Eynon and his team at ISEAL are currently looking to prove the same link in humans. As he puts it, "We think you need this protein to sprint very fast." About 16 percent of humans are naturally deficient. In contrast, among 300 world-class sprinters, Eynon and his colleagues found that deficiency approaches 0 percent, although it accounts for just 1 to 1.5 percent of the variance in total sprinting ability. "All that we can say with a very high level of certainty about this gene is that if you are deficient in it, you probably will not be an elite sprinter," Eynon says.

Making It Happen

In addition to fitness levels, scientists have found telling mental traits that differentiate top athletes from amateurs. First, those competing at the national or international level appear to have more experiences of what is described as flow—a state of deep absorption in an activity during which performance seems to happen effortlessly and automatically. They are also more likely to feel something trainers call "making it happen"—involving intense focus and effort under pressure. Researchers suspect that athletes are not only better at channeling these mental states naturally but that they also sharpen them by having ample opportunity to experience them.

"There are certainly times athletes can win without experiencing flow or making it happen," says sports psychology researcher Christian Swann of the University of Wollongong in Australia. "But when they do something excellent that they perceive as being close to their best performance, typically it will involve one of those states and sometimes both." Swann and his colleagues are writing up new findings indicating that specific personality traits—including confidence, competitiveness, adaptive perfectionism (a form that relishes achievement while tolerating mistakes and avoiding self-criticism), optimism and mental toughness—seem to predispose individuals to achieving flow states.

Athletes also excel at certain perceptual and cognitive tasks. In 2013 Heloisa Alves, a cognitive neuroscientist then at the University of Illinois at Urbana-Champaign, and her colleagues recruited 87 elite Brazilian volleyball players and 67 matched controls to perform a number of tests of executive control, memory and visuospatial attention. Compared with nonathletes, the volleyball players demonstrated faster reaction times in two executive-control tasks and one visuospatial-attentional processing task, as well as greater mental control.

"Our basic understanding is that longtime physical training, specifically in sports, also involves some cognitive training, including attention and executive control," Alves says. "So when you become an elite athlete, you somehow become an expert in certain cognitive abilities as well."

The highest echelon of sportsmen and sportswomen may also have additional psychological differences, according to scientists who conducted studies for UK Sport, a governmental organization that promotes elite sports and athletic development. Specifically, UK Sport asked researchers to elucidate the fine-grained differences between elite athletes—professionals who compete at the Olympics or other major championships but who usually do not take home a major medal—and the so-called superelites who consistently win. UK Sport hoped to use its findings to foster more superelites and increase Britain's Olympic prowess.

Sports psychologist Tim Woodman and his colleagues at Bangor University in Wales, collaborating with other universities and UK Sport, took up the effort, recruiting 32 male and female British athletes: 16 superelites who had won two to 18 medals each, including at least one gold, at major world championships, and 16 matched elites, who had never won a medal but had competed at the same level. The researchers interviewed the participants, their coaches and their parents, asking questions about the athletes' life histories. Because these interviews generated more than 8,400 pages of data, the researchers turned to a novel pattern-recognition program to identify differences among the groups.

What they found took them by surprise. "There's a long-standing view that happiness makes people achieve, but this study blows that assumption out of the water," Woodman says. "Not only is happiness not the key, but it doesn't feature anywhere along the way." Indeed, the team found that all of the superelites had experienced a critical negative event—their parents' divorce, a death, disease or some other perceived loss—early in life. And shortly after, all managed to discover sports, which they uniformly recalled as a highly positive turn, changing their course almost immediately. "Suddenly they felt valued, important and inspired, perhaps for the first time," says Matthew Barlow, a postdoctoral researcher in sports psychology at Bangor who collaborated with Woodman.

Men and Women of Steel

Early trauma and recovery through sports were not all that Woodman and his colleagues found when they examined the life stories of superelite athletes. Very often these individuals had experienced another critical turning point later on in their sporting career. Whether this event was positive, like switching to an inspirational new coach, or negative, like the death of a loved one, it caused the athletes to redouble their efforts. "This big midcareer event reminds them of that original loss and motivates them at a deep-seated level," Barlow theorizes.

This common narrative—from a loss to sports to deeper motivation—seems to shape the personality and outlook of superelites in predictable ways. For starters, Woodman says, "the importance of not losing is very keen." Superelite athletes often express an obsessive need to win, as opposed to a desire for fame, happiness or money, which motivates many of their less successful competitors.

They are also "far more ruthless and selfish in their approach to their sport," Woodman explains, not hesitating, for example, to split up with a spouse or partner if they think the relationship compromises their goals. And while less successful elite athletes tend to focus on beating opponents, the superelites put equal value on beating themselves and others. As Woodman says, "They always thought they could do better, no matter how well they performed."

Woodman and his team have presented their findings at UK Sport's annual World Class Performance Conference and plan to publish all their results later this year. Overall, he says, their study implies that those who do not experience a traumatic event early in life "are less likely to have the drive necessary for that obsessive level of achievement." No one is suggesting that coaches traumatize their protégés in hopes of unleashing a superelite, but there are some actionable lessons, Woodman notes. For example, talent scouts looking to develop Olympic athletes could keep an eye out for promising candidates "who had a rough ride somewhere along the way."

Eynon stresses that no matter how far work progresses on the genetics and other determinants of elite performance, the findings should never be used to exclude people, with coaches selecting only those with the most biological promise. If that seems far-fetched, there are already a few companies selling direct-to-consumer genetic tests. These products purport to identify sprinting and aerobic ability from DNA in saliva samples, but, Eynon says, all are based on weak science. He also notes that not all serious athletes are elite, especially in team sports, so even if a test for elite potential did exist, it should not be used as a deterrent for playing sports.

"There are players who really shine," Eynon says, "and ones who help. Don't you ever stop doing sports on the basis of a genetic test." If nothing else, taking part in a sport that you love gives you a deeper appreciation of those athletes who are able to compete among the world's best.

About the Author

Rachel Nuwer is a freelance journalist and author of Poached: Inside the Dark World of Wildlife Trafficking *(Da Capo Press, 2018). She lives in Brooklyn, N.Y.*

How Olympic Figure Skaters Break Records with Physics

By Tanya Lewis

Today's figure skaters are performing feats of athletic prowess that were unimaginable only a few decades ago. At the Winter Olympics in Beijing last week, U.S. skater Nathan Chen took home the gold with short program and free skate performances packed with quadruple jumps and triple Axels. And 15-year-old Russian skater Kamila Valieva became the first woman to land a quadruple jump—actually two—in Olympic competition in the mixed-gender team event. (According to news reports, Valieva has tested positive for a banned substance, the heart drug trimetazidine.) Quadruple jumps, or quads, involve launching off the ice, completing at least four revolutions in the air and landing on one foot. Such achievements require exquisite strength, speed and grace—but the physics behind them is fairly straightforward.

Figure skating features roughly half a dozen types of jumps. They differ by which part of the skate's blade one jumps off of (the front, also called the "toe pick," or the inner or outer edge) and the number of revolutions made in the air (single, double, triple or quad). Toe jumps include the flip, Lutz and toe loop. Edge jumps include the loop, Salchow and Axel.

Quad jumps—including quad Salchows and quad toe loops—have become common in the men's competition (most of the top male skaters do them), and a number of women have landed them in competitions outside of the Olympics or in practice. The quadruple Axel is generally considered the most challenging jump because it requires a forward takeoff and four and a half rotations in the air. To date, no one of any gender has successfully completed a quad Axel in competition, although skaters such as Japan's Yuzuru Hanyu have tried. And some experts think a quint—a quintuple, or five-revolution, jump—is theoretically within reach.

15

Deborah King, a professor of exercise science and athletic training at Ithaca College, studies the physics of figure skating. *Scientific American* spoke with her about how skaters perform these feats of agility, the physical boundaries of the sport and how today's Olympic athletes are expanding them.

[An edited transcript of the interview follows.]

How did you get into studying figure skating?

I did my master's in exercise science at the University of Massachusetts Amherst and didn't really know what I wanted to do for a career after that, besides biomechanics in sports and exercise. There was a position open at the Olympic Training Center in Colorado Springs, Colo., in its sports science and technology division. When I was there, there was a figure skating camp. And one of the coaches that was there was really interested in studying the biomechanics of the triple Axel. So that pretty much launched my work into figure skating biomechanics—it was a really cool project. I had no experience with figure skating before that.

Can you explain the physics behind the main types of jumps?

Regardless of the figure skating technique that makes one jump different from the other, there are some basic physics that are common to all of them. From a pure mechanical standpoint, skaters, without a doubt, have to be in the air long enough to complete however many revolutions they're trying to do. To get the time in the air for the jumps, that is related to jump height—and that is pretty much related to how much vertical velocity they can get when they jump off the ice. Depending on whether it's a toe pick jump or an edge jump, the movement patterns they do to get that vertical velocity will differ.

For toe pick jumps, you're sort of vaulting off the toe pick to pop up. And the edge jumps, it's more like you extend your leg and maybe use your arms a little bit to get some of that vertical velocity. Particularly for the toe pick jumps, the horizontal velocity you have can be used to do more like a pole-vaulting-type motion. In that case, extra horizontal speed could be helpful to store more energy in your leg. You're coming in with this sort of linear momentum, but as you rotate over the leg, that horizontal motion is actually now being redirected a little vertically. It's called tangential velocity. So, certainly, horizontal velocity can be helpful for generating vertical velocity. Horizontal speed is probably not going to help as much for an edge jump—you're mostly just pushing off and generally getting work out of your muscles.

Why are these jumps so difficult to perform?

Skaters have got two things that they need to do at once, which makes it really hard: They need to spring off the ice—that's going to give them that vertical velocity for the height—and they need to start rotating really fast. As they're pressing off the ice to go up into the air, they also need to be creating the torque [a type of rotational force] against the ice, which is going to give them rotational momentum. They need that rotation momentum so that when they come off the ice, they can pull into a really tight position and rotate really fast.

Is this like when one spins in an office chair and brings in their arms to spin faster?

Exactly, the actual physics behind that is: you're reducing your moment of inertia, which increases your rotational velocity.

What do skaters need to do to complete more rotations during a jump?

To do quad jumps, compared with triple jumps, for most skaters, it comes down to rotational speed. From a theoretical standpoint, extra height will help. Skaters doing quads generally have higher jumps.

Is there a fundamental limit to how many spins a skater can do?

I absolutely think people could do quintuple jumps. But there is only so much strength a person can have—and power they can produce—as they jump off the ice to get so high. Even if you think of the vertical jump record at the [National Football League

Scouting] Combine, people are not jumping two to three meters in the air. And you can only get so narrow. You're limited by the breadth of your shoulders and hips—you can only get down to a certain minimum moment of inertia based on your specific anthropometry [body proportions].

The other factor where skaters could potentially improve—in order to do more rotations—would be rotational momentum as they come off the ice. As they do their approach or footwork into the takeoff, they create torque about the rotating axis as they push off the ice. If they can get more rotational momentum as they're still exploding upward, then they can rotate faster with that small body position. It's sort of like: if you're on a tire swing, and someone pushes you harder, you're going to rotate faster. So there are three things you can play with.

Skaters should be mathematically able to do a quint Salchow or toe loop. A quad Axel is, to me, probably the limit because it is 4.5 revolutions.

Do male skaters have an advantage over female ones when it comes to doing more rotations?

Generally, you're seeing just the differences in muscle mass between male and female skaters. Obviously, there's overlap, and the top end of the female skaters flow over into the male ones. But if you look at the bell curves of strength and power, you do have greater strength and power from most male skaters. Most of the male skaters are jumping a little higher than the female ones, and most of them are likely going to be able to generate more rotational momentum coming off the ice. You could [argue male skaters have] a disadvantage in that, generally speaking, they're not going to be able to get as tight or as small a moment of inertia. So it can be harder for the guys because, generally, skaters tend to be petite.

Is there an optimal age for figure skating?

In terms of women, you see lot of skaters hitting their jumps before puberty. It can be particularly hard for female skaters when they go through puberty because changes in your body size and shape make you have to relearn your jumps. It also happens to men, but that's probably more a result of a mismatch in growth spurts because the muscles have to keep up.

In the 1998 Winter Olympics in Nagano, Japan, French figure skater Surya Bonaly performed an impressive—and technically illegal—backflip on the ice. How did she achieve that?

It's kind of the same basic physical principles as other jumps. The rotation's about a different axis. As opposed to the vertical axis involved in most figure skating jumps, she was rotating about what a lot of people call the flip, or the tumbling, axis. When you're watching gymnasts, they go more head over heals. Some of the same principles are involved—for example, you need to be high enough that your body rotates over [for one backflip]. Gymnasts do, like, double backflips. But you could not see, off of ice, a triple or quadruple backflip. Landing on ice is also difficult. If you come up short, it's not a particularly forgiving surface.

Ouch, I can imagine. What impact—quite literally—do all these jumps have on the body?

We're trying to look at the forces involved in landing. Not a lot of people have done that yet. There's not a lot of ready-tailored equipment that can be attached to a skate. My colleagues at Brigham Young University and I instrumented a figure skating blade with sensors that would measure force. When we got it calibrated, COVID hit. So we haven't actually measured the forces yet.

We have some ideas of how big we think the forces are. Most people would say the landings are somewhere between five to six times body weight, up to maybe 10 to 12 times body weight. And it's all on one foot, too. It's a lot of abuse on the same leg, over and over again, on a really hard surface. Skaters do have a lot of injuries. If you watch it on TV, it looks so graceful, easy and beautiful. But if you go to the edge of a rink while they're practicing, you can hear the sound of the takeoffs and the landings, and you quickly get an impression of the magnitude of impact forces.

About the Author

Tanya Lewis is a senior editor at Scientific American *who covers health and medicine.*

Hormone Levels Are Being Used to Discriminate Against Female Athletes

By Grace Huckins

In February 2016 Dutee Chand became the best woman sprinter in India. The record she set on an indoor track in Qatar during a qualifying heat stands as the fastest time an Indian woman has ever achieved in the 60-meter race, and she soon became the first Indian woman in decades to race the 100 meters at the Olympics. Just a year earlier, however, Chand had faced the possibility of never again running competitively.

In 2014, as Chand was making her mark on the junior-level track world, the Athletics Federation of India (AFI), with the support of its international parent body World Athletics, barred her from competing in women's events because of atypically high levels of testosterone occurring naturally in her body. (There is no evidence Chand ever took banned substances to alter her hormones.) According to the AFI, which runs India's track-and-field competitions, her higher-than-average testosterone level gave her physical advantages enjoyed by male athletes. Chand disputed the idea that this hyperandrogenism—an elevated level of androgens, the class of hormones that includes testosterone—made her more like a male sprinter than a female one, and in 2015 the Court of Arbitration for Sport agreed with her. It determined that World Athletics, which sets the rules governing international track-and-field competitions, had not presented enough scientific evidence to defend its claims—and Chand could run again.

But World Athletics now contends that it has found an adequate scientific basis for barring women with high testosterone from competing in races between 400 meters and one mile unless they take medication to lower their testosterone levels or opt to compete against men. This policy does not apply to Chand, because she runs shorter distances, but it could end the athletic dreams of Mokgadi

Caster Semenya, an Olympic gold medalist and a hero in her home country of South Africa. In 2019 the Court of Arbitration for Sport accepted World Athletics' argument, and the Swiss Supreme Court upheld this decision in September 2020. Rather than undergo medically unnecessary treatment to suppress her testosterone levels, Semenya has decided to compete only in the 200-meter race, an event without limits on testosterone levels, at the 2021 Tokyo Olympics.

This sequence of controversial decisions has prompted a public debate about fairness and discrimination in sports. Throughout the Olympics' modern history, rules about who counts as a woman have shifted as the scientific understanding of sex has progressed. Disqualifying athletes on the basis of natural testosterone levels is one of the last legal forms of discrimination in sports.

As an interdisciplinary scholar trained in both biology and gender studies, I have examined the ways in which scientists take social categories such as "woman" and "man" and attempt to turn them into fundamental truths. For as long as scientists have been trying to figure out the biological basis of sex and gender, nature has presented divergences from their theories. ("Sex" refers to biological characteristics; "gender" refers to social roles and identification.)

Most men have XY chromosomes and developed testicles in utero that, later in life, secrete relatively high amounts of testosterone into their bloodstreams. In contrast, most women have XX chromosomes, which drives the production of ovaries and lower levels of testosterone. Some women, however, have XY chromosomes as well as external female anatomy; these women are affected by the World Athletics policy. Such attributes reflecting variation beyond the rigid male/female binary are known as intersex traits.

According to interAct, an intersex advocacy organization, 1.7 percent of the population may be intersex, although many never realize it. And they may be overrepresented in the world of elite sports: in its published decision, the Court of Arbitration for Sport repeatedly referenced the statistic that among elite athletes, women with XY chromosomes are far more common than they are in the general population.

It seems, then, that intersex women may have an edge in athletic competitions. But so, too, do athletes with natural advantages such as, say, height in basketball tournaments. The important question here is not whether some sex traits can confer athletic advantages but whether those advantages are so meaningful and so incontrovertible that they should prevent a woman athlete such as Semenya from competing against other women.

Chromosomes and Hormones

Sex has never been a simple binary. Nevertheless, Olympic regulators have tried for decades to apply overly simplistic rules to this messy reality. From the 1960s until the 1990s dozens of women were singled out and even disqualified because of their chromosomes. The first was Ewa Kłobukowska, who was deemed a woman based on genital examination in 1966 but was disqualified from the 1968 Olympics because of her XY chromosomal makeup. Kłobukowska's story is not so surprising: Some intersex women are anatomically so similar to other women that they never discover their XY chromosomal makeup.

Chromosomal testing thus disqualified some people who had every trait of the female sex except for XX chromosomes. This contradiction, coupled with the invasiveness of some testing and the dire social consequences for those who failed the tests, eventually led the International Olympic Committee to abandon sex testing in the 1990s. But its concern about ensuring the apparent fairness of women's competitions did not disappear, and it reserved for itself the option to test people on a case-by-case basis. Recent cases of sex testing have focused not on chromosomes but on an aspect of sex ostensibly more related to athletic ability: testosterone levels.

Athletes have been using artificial testosterone since at least the 1950s in the hopes of improving their performance, but until the 1990s the medical community did not hold that the link between supplemental testosterone and athletic ability had adequate scientific support. That might have influenced the International Olympic

23

Committee's choice not to use testosterone levels in its sex-verification era. The paradigm changed after 1996, when a study demonstrated that testosterone supplementation, in combination with weight training, could increase both muscle size and strength in men.

Since then, endocrinologists have greatly expanded their understanding of the relation between testosterone and muscle mass. The evidence shows that testosterone both increases the number of muscle cells that the body produces and enhances muscle size. There is some evidence that testosterone may also influence athletic ability through other mechanisms. In one experiment, men who took high levels of testosterone (but not those who took lower levels) had increased levels of hemoglobin in their bloodstreams, a change that allows blood to carry more oxygen to the rest of the body. Testosterone could also exert influence on bone mass because low testosterone levels, much like low estrogen levels, are correlated with osteoporosis, and both hormones have a role in maintaining bone structure.

In fact, androgens ("male" hormones, including testosterone) and estrogens ("female" hormones) are much more tightly linked than most people imagine. For starters, everyone naturally produces both hormones. And all naturally occurring estrogen in humans was once testosterone, transformed into estrogen by the enzyme aromatase. Scientists debate how much of a given hormone is "normal" and how those levels should be measured—one recent study even concluded that "normal" testosterone levels for women should be adjusted to better accommodate female athletes. And men's and women's estrogen levels can actually overlap, especially during some phases of the menstrual cycle. Even so, testosterone levels do vary considerably between men and women: younger men's levels tend to range between 10 and 40 nanomoles per liter of blood, whereas women's levels tend to range between 0.5 and 3 nmol/L.

Taken together, the available evidence—the gap in between most men's and women's testosterone levels, the established connection between testosterone doping and increased muscle mass, and the approximately 10 percent advantage that elite men have over elite women in track events—seems to imply that women with high testosterone levels will run like men. Nevertheless in Chand's case, the Court of Arbitration for Sport found that she could not be banned from competition, because there was not yet any direct evidence of the relation between natural testosterone levels and athletic ability in elite women.

The court decided differently in Semenya's case four years later, partly because it believed that such evidence had been produced. Stéphane Bermon, head of World Athletics' scientific team, had recently published a paper that analyzed data from two international athletics competitions and found that women with higher levels of testosterone performed better, on average, than women with lower levels. Because this study is based on real-world data from elite female runners, it arguably represents the most relevant findings in the hyperandrogenism controversy to date.

I spend some of my research time trawling the scientific literature to find cases of researchers making statistical errors, particularly when their studies pertain to marginalized groups. So I was intrigued to read that a group of scientists had questioned the validity of this key study on the basis of issues with the data. In response to their concerns, Bermon updated the study, and although he still observed some effects, his conclusion was markedly weakened by the correction. When I performed a procedure called correcting for multiple comparisons—a statistical method that takes into account the increased probability of finding at least one false positive when many statistical tests, as opposed to only one, are conducted—on his reported results, these effects disappeared.

This complication does not imply that there is no relation between testosterone and athletic performance in women. What is certainly the case, however, is that far more research is needed before a firm conclusion can be reached.

Supplemental Is Not Natural

If testosterone taken illegally and testosterone produced naturally had the same impact on all bodies, one would assume that male-typical levels of testosterone necessarily confer a male-typical athletic advantage. But to understand what such studies mean for women like Semenya, we must understand how their bodies work. All the women targeted by World Athletics' policy on testosterone levels are intersex, with a similar set of sex traits: they have XY chromosomes, but their bodies do not respond to androgens in the same way most XY individuals do. Because of the complexity inherent in the function of hormones, it is extremely difficult to determine the precise effect that testosterone will have on these intersex people.

Even if androgens did have a completely typical effect on them, the link between testosterone and athletic ability would remain far more tenuous than it might seem. Taking *supplemental* testosterone may tend to give someone bigger muscles, but that does not automatically imply that a person with *naturally* higher testosterone levels will be better at sports than someone with lower testosterone levels. Even the original, contested version of Bermon's study hints at a nuanced connection: whereas testosterone showed a positive effect on athletic ability for a couple of events, no effect was observed for 16 other events, and the data suggested that higher testosterone levels may be associated with worse performance in several events.

One study of elite Swedish athletes found no association between testosterone and athletic performance, and a recent study of teenage athletes in Australia showed a strong negative correlation between testosterone levels in women and performance. Men, too, do not necessarily gain an enormous advantage from high testosterone levels: almost 17 percent of elite male athletes measured in one study had testosterone levels below the typical male range, and nearly 10 percent of them had testosterone levels under 5 nmol/L.

The clear effect of testosterone supplements on the body and the average differences in muscle mass between men and women make it easy to assume that higher testosterone levels automatically confer superior athletic ability regardless of other factors. But the science shows that, at least among elite athletes, the link between testosterone and athletic performance is far from straightforward.

One of the first things a person learns when studying the science of sex and gender is how difficult it is to disentangle biological and social influences. For me, this issue came into stark relief when I studied apparently sex-linked advantages in areas such as spatial ability. Because men tend to experience both higher levels of testosterone and more encouragement in STEM fields than do their female counterparts, it is difficult to determine whether biological or social factors cause these differences. To answer these questions, scientists study people who have high testosterone and do not experience a masculine social environment—that is, women with particular intersex traits—and examine their behavior to differentiate between biological and social causes.

The story gets far more convoluted when we try not only to distinguish between biological and social causes but also to investigate how those factors interact. One fascinating example comes from the work of neuroscientist Melissa Hines, who studied girls with congenital adrenal hyperplasia, a condition in which intersex traits arise in XX females because of unusually high levels of androgens. Hines showed that these girls tend to engage in play behavior seen relatively more often in boys, such as horseplay. More recently, however, she demonstrated that the girls do not necessarily prefer horseplay over dolls: they just do not care about what other girls tend to do. Most young girls will prefer to play with a red ball over a blue ball if they see that other girls are playing only with red balls, but girls with congenital adrenal hyperplasia will happily play with either toy. Testosterone does not make girls more likely to wrestle than to read; it simply changes the extent to which they respond to social cues about gender.

In terms of its effects on behavior, testosterone is thus quite complex: it seems to work together with social cues such that neither factor can be isolated from the other. Although these apparently psychological observations may be irrelevant to the question of athletic ability, even Bermon and his colleagues have suggested that dominance and aggression, long associated with testosterone levels, could have a role in winning races. In one of the only studies that systematically examined the effect of taking testosterone on women's physical ability, those who took high levels of the hormone saw modestly increased muscle mass and dramatically increased strength. The researchers hypothesized that some unmeasured psychological factor allowed their slightly more developed muscles to make extraordinary athletic gains.

But it is also far too simplistic to assume that testosterone causes aggression or competitiveness, even though women might be more likely to enter competitive situations when their testosterone levels are higher, and men who respond more strongly to androgens might be more confident about their chances in competition. In fact, numerous studies have demonstrated that a person's testosterone levels will increase after, rather than before, they have won a competition or otherwise shown dominance, and one 2015 study suggested that this effect might be stronger in women than it is in men. Behavior, which is affected by social norms about men and women, exerts an influence on hormone levels—demonstrating yet again the intricate and perhaps inextricable links between the social and the biological.

When critics argue that intersex women are basically "biological men" who just happen to have clitorises and labia, they are completely neglecting the enormous influences that the categories "men" and "women" have on all of our lives—and on all of our bodies. Testosterone is not some mysterious entity that comes from nowhere to exert a huge influence on our bodies and our minds: it both changes and is changed by gender norms.

Despite being just a single element in a knotty, sometimes circular network of factors that contribute to athletic ability, testosterone is unlikely to be completely irrelevant. Somehow XY women seem likelier to achieve physical feats than XX women. This observation does not imply, however, that intersex women should be forced to compete in the men's category against men, against whom they will surely lose. Arguing that biology instructs us to divide athletes at a threshold of five nanomoles of testosterone per liter of blood, as World Athletics has done, implies that this threshold splits humans into the two fairest, most equal competitive groups possible.

Given that testosterone affects athletic ability in a complex, nonlinear fashion, this suggestion is not supported by the evidence. It would be far more sensible to split basketball into two separate height divisions: no current player in the NBA is shorter than 5'9", whereas both low-testosterone men and low-testosterone women can be extremely successful athletes. Nor is there any cogent reason to identify intersex conditions as conferring unique genetic advantages in a domain such as elite athletics, where a variety of unusual traits lead to success. Why should swimmer Michael Phelps's low lactic acid production (which helps stave off muscle fatigue) or the late NBA player Manute Bol's uncommon height be rewarded while Semenya's somewhat higher testosterone level is disqualifying?

If biology cannot give us a firm basis for dividing athletes into two distinct categories, we might wonder why we have men's and women's divisions at all. Although testosterone levels might not divide all of humanity neatly into better and worse athletes, it is the case that, at the most elite level, men outperform women in sports such as track. Making sports coed and thus de facto barring women from Olympic races would not be intrinsically unfair—after all, plenty of groups of people, such as those with poor cardiovascular health, can never dream of becoming elite runners—but it would be regrettable. We would lose women such as sprinter Allyson Felix, swimmer Katie Ledecky and the extraordinary U.S. women's soccer squad, all of whom inspire countless young women.

Biology alone is too limited a tool to tell us how to divide up the athletic field—but it can help us gain a greater understanding of natural human variation. Particularly in a domain as convoluted and controversial as sex and gender, science often uncovers more ambiguity than it resolves. And if science does not inform the issue of intersex women in sports, we can still revert to the values of diversity, inclusion and acceptance that make elite women's sports so extraordinary in the first place.

About the Author

Grace Huckins is a doctoral student in neuroscience at Stanford University and a graduate of the master's programs in neuroscience and women's studies at the University of Oxford.

Elite Athletes' Gut Bacteria Give Rodent Runners a Boost

By Emily Willingham

Doping scandals have rocked the world of athletics competitions repeatedly. Lance Armstrong's dramatic fall took his seven Tour de France titles with it, and the BALCO scandal embroiled athletes from professional baseball and football and Olympic track-and-field sports. More recently, the International Association of Athletics Federations, which governs track competitions globally, drew fire after it required Olympic running champion Caster Semenya to medically reduce her testosterone levels if she wanted to compete.

This tension between "antidoping" agencies and elite athletes may notch up a level if findings reported on June 24 in *Nature Medicine* keep their performance-enhancing promise. Researchers say that proportions of certain bacterial species increase after endurance athletes have completed a marathon. Furthermore, they say, these bacteria break down lactate, also known as lactic acid, which is notorious for bringing on shaky legs after intense exertion. In doing so, they produce another compound, propionate, that might boost endurance.

The study began with an assessment of 15 runners and a comparison of bacterial strains present in their stool before and after they completed the Boston Marathon. The investigators identified a boost in the presence of the species of bacterium *Veillonella* after the marathon, especially *Veillonella atypica*. They also found that these bacteria were more abundant in the marathoners as compared with 10 nonathletes. These bacteria use lactate and break it down into propionate.

Moving on to another group of athletes, ultramarathoners and Olympic trial rowers, the researchers got similar results: higher levels of *Veillonella* after an endurance competition. They also found that following the intense physical activity, stool samples from these

31

athletes had higher levels of every bacterial gene involved in breaking down lactate to propionate.

Intrigued by their findings in people, study author George Church, a genetics professor at Harvard University, and his colleagues turned to mice to see what dosing with *Veillonella* or propionate would do to the animals' treadmill performance. Oral *Veillonella* boosted rodent endurance on the treadmill, and rectal administration of propionate did so as well. In addition, the investigators established that lactate can cross from the blood into the gut, where *Veillonella* might act as a kind of lactate sponge.

The findings are intriguing and support the idea that such bacterial activity can affect exercise function, says Fergus Shanahan, a professor and chair of the department of medicine at University College Cork in Ireland, who was not involved in the work. But he cautions that among elite athletes, these responses likely appear late in the process of becoming superfit and are not necessarily something anyone would see with short-term physical activity.

"Of course, elite athletes will be tempted to leverage this new information to achieve even marginal gain," Shanahan says, "but we know too little about the microbiome to advocate such a strategy." Exercise physiologists might want to expand their horizons and consider host-microbe interactions in light of the findings, he adds.

Church says that the next steps include applying a similar approach to evaluate many other biochemicals that are linked to the action of microbes in the gut, some of which might affect immunity or neurological function. In addition to "many experiments left to do," he says, the researchers are planning to pursue a version of the mouse treadmill study in people.

Church and lead study author Jonathan Scheiman are among the founders of the start-up Fitbiomics. A preliminary version of the findings was presented in 2017 at the American Chemical Society's national meeting. At that time, Scheiman said in a statement that he hoped the team would have "a novel probiotic on the market" within a year after the company's launch—a product that has yet to come to market.

The results of these investigations captured the attention of officials at antidoping agencies. "We will continue to eagerly follow those outcomes," says Matt Fedoruk, chief science officer at the U.S. Anti-Doping Agency, particularly for whether they "unfairly influence competitive results." Right now, he says, the study is an important first step in identifying possible links between gut bacteria and athletic performance.

The World Anti-Doping Agency (WADA) says that the expert group that develops its "Prohibited List" of substances has yet to even discuss the potential performance-enhancing effects of gut microbiota species and their metabolites. James Fitzgerald, a spokesperson for the agency, says that the list evolves based on new findings and that WADA will pay close attention.

Church, meanwhile, has a different perspective. "Hopefully people will enjoy the pure science for now," he says, "and keep an eye out for future rigorous clinical trials on consuming specific microbes or biochemicals."

About the Author

Emily Willingham is a science writer and author of Phallacy: Life Lessons from the Animal Penis *(Avery, Penguin Publishing Group, 2020) and* The Tailored Brain: From Ketamine, to Keto, to Companionship: A User's Guide to Feeling Better and Thinking Smarter *(Basic Books, 2021).*

Four Myths About Testosterone

By Rebecca M. Jordan-Young and Katrina Karkazis

I n May of this year, the sports world's self-appointed judiciary, the international Court of Arbitration for Sport (CAS), upheld a controversial regulation that prevents women with naturally high testosterone (T) from competing in the women's category in long sprint and middle distance running events. South African middle-distance runner Caster Semenya brought the case, with Athletics South Africa, against the International Association of Athletics Federations (IAAF), arguing that IAAF's rule is unscientific, unethical and discriminatory.

The CAS panel affirmed that the rule is discriminatory because it only applies to the women's category, and only to some women within that category. But in a two-to-one decision, CAS deemed the discrimination to be "justified" based on the IAAF's arguments about sex differences and T. Men are, on average across athletics events, 9–12 percent better than women. The IAAF claims that T is "the main driver" of this difference. By extension, it also claims that women with T levels in the typical male range have an "insuperable advantage" over women with T in the typical female range.

While this case raises important questions of ethics, human rights and medical harm, the IAAF defends the rule with claims about scientific consensus, glossing over profound disagreements about the evidence. Here, we address four myths central to these debates.

Myth 1: T is the "master molecule of athleticism."

T's effect on athletic performance isn't always positive, as the IAAF's own data on elite women athletes well demonstrates. Its initial analysis of data from two world championship competitions showed that women with higher T had significantly better performances in only five of 21 events.

Serious methodological problems with the IAAF paper prompted independent researchers to call for the paper's retraction, and the IAAF issued a correction. But the corrected version still undermines the regulation. In three of 11 running events, the *lowest T* group did better, and the strongest association across all events was the *negative* association between T and performance in the 100 meters, where lower T athletes ran 5.4 percent faster than the highest T athletes. In none of the events where high T athletes performed better was the gap greater than 2.9 percent.

One independent group requested and obtained a subset of the IAAF data, concluding: "The results of [the IAAF's first study] are clearly unreliable, and those of [the second study] are of unknown validity," making it "impossible" to discern the real relationship, if any, between T and performance. Clearly, though, neither this study nor the broader sports science literature support the IAAF's claim that targeted athletes "have the same advantages over [other] women as men do over women."

Many studies across a range of sports show similar mixed relationships between performance and T. Consider a recent analysis of teenage Olympic weightlifters, in which the best predictor of strength was lean body mass, which has a complicated relationship to T. Among girls, body mass was initially the only significant predictor of weightlifting performance, and T was a predictor of body mass. But, counterintuitively, once the investigators controlled for the girls' size, they unmasked a strong *negative* relationship between T levels and performance: girls with *lower* T lifted more weight.

The researchers noted that T affects muscle, which is crucial to force, but T also affects breast tissue and fat localization in the lower limbs; the latter may be especially important for certain powerlifting moves. Controlling for body mass, there were *no* relationships between any hormones and performance in boys, even though their T levels ranged from 0.5 to 30.2 nanomoles per liter. In short, T (and other steroids) affect multiple body systems, and the relationships sometimes work in a positive synergy to improve performance, but they sometimes detract from performance.

Myth 2: The best way to see what T does for athletic performance is to compare men and women.

It's simple, some people argue: men have "greater lean body mass (more skeletal muscle and less fat), larger hearts (both in absolute terms and scaled to lean body mass), higher cardiac outputs, larger hemoglobin mass, larger VO2 max (a person's ability to take in oxygen), greater glycogen utilization and higher anaerobic capacity"; these all affect athletic performance, and are all affected by T, so men's greater athletic performance must be due to their higher average T levels.

This is a series of linked, but not necessarily logically connected propositions. The wide range of physiological and social differences between women and men athletes confound those comparisons. Even characteristics that are influenced by T are also affected by multiple other factors. They can't simply be boiled down to T, either in adulthood or during earlier development.

Scientists overwhelmingly prefer within-sex comparisons to answer most questions about the factors influencing sports performance, though sometimes it's useful to analyze data both within and across sexes. Emerging research using both types of analysis reveals that some factors long thought to be fundamentally sex- differentiated turn out to hinge on other elements. For instance, most studies have shown that men have a greater proportion of fast-twitch muscle fibers, a difference traditionally attributed to genetics.

A recent study of elite weightlifters, though, found women had as many, or more, fast-twitch fibers as men, and concluded that "athlete caliber and/or years competing in the sport influence [muscle fiber proportion] more than sex per se." T also likely has a relationship with fiber type via body mass, but as the teenage weightlifter study shows, the relationship with T and body mass isn't straightforward. Simple comparisons of women and men athletes can't reveal the specific relationships that underlie athletes' physiologies, and can obscure the recursive, sometimes positive and sometimes negative relationships with T that are in the mix.

Myth 3: Suppressing an athlete's T reduces performance, so different T levels between athletes must similarly affect performance.

The IAAF says it has data showing women athletes' performance suffers following abrupt and dramatic T suppression. While this may be true, the organization isn't justified in using this observation to conclude that women with higher T levels "possess a very clear performance advantage" over their peers, on par with what men typically have over women.

The IAAF narrative suggests that manipulating T only affects athletically-relevant aspects of function, disregarding the fatigue, sleep disturbance, metabolic changes and other physical problems that accompany significant hormonal disruption. The drop in performance might be attributable to these many side effects, physiological changes and psychological influences.

Moreover, manipulating T in individuals can't illuminate how T levels figure in differences across athletes: this confuses intra-individual analysis for inter-individual analysis. There's not just a logical problem with this conflation, but a data problem, which P.J. Vazel, an elite track and field coach and member of the Association of Track and Field Statisticians, underscores when he notes that in individuals, "raising or lowering T will show a relationship with performance," but in analyses across athletes, often "there is no relationship found with performance."

Faryal Mirza, a clinical endocrinologist at the University of Connecticut Medical Center, suggested that one reason studies don't always find consistent links between T level and physiological variables is that sometimes high T signals that a person isn't very efficient at using T: the body is producing more precisely to arrive at "typical" function. (Faryal Mirza, conversation with the authors.)

37

Myth 4: These regulations are solely about T and performance.

Scientific claims are central to this debate, but so is the broader context in which IAAF officials communicate their beliefs about women's bodies. The vehicle for performance differences is supposed to be T but, as the IAAF has been forced repeatedly to defend the T regulations, it has revealed its concern lies less with the T level than with the source of the T.

The IAAF has made this concern explicit by narrowing the group of women to whom the regulations apply. Women with polycystic ovarian syndrome (PCOS), the most common reason that women have naturally high T levels, and congenital adrenal hyperplasia (CAH) were recently explicitly excluded from the 2019 regulations even when their levels exceed the threshold, though the IAAF has argued that women with PCOS and CAH derive "advantage" from high T.

Likewise, recent IAAF statements highlight sex-atypical chromosomes and gonads, which functions as a dog whistle to suggest that the targeted women athletes are not "really" women. Yet this rule was supposed to be different from prior sex testing regulations, precisely because it focused on T rather than on other aspects of sex biology that are variable among women (and men). Even for those who accept that endogenous T makes an outsized contribution to athletic performance, the defining feature is supposed to be the level of T, not the source of it.

The IAAF's enforcement of gender normativity is also evident in its rebuttal of concerns raised by the World Medical Association and the United Nations, among others, about mandating that healthy athletes undergo medically unnecessary interventions in order to compete. Rather than viewing the serious and long-term consequences of lowering testosterone as "side effects," the IAAF proposes that they are "the desired effects." These changes—including reduced muscle and increased fat—are supposed to produce the kind of body that Stéphane Bermon, Director of the IAAF Health and Science Department, has presented as the "ideal female phenotype" at scientific conferences.

Disregarding women athletes who have resisted these interventions, even to the point of bringing legal challenges against the regulation, the IAAF insists that these "medications are gender-affirming" and "change their body to better reflect their chosen gender." The latter statement insinuates that women athletes who do not willingly modify their bodies to fit IAAF standards actively "choose" their gender, which deliberately encourages confusion with transgender athletes.

These four myths are subtle yet powerful. Owing to the ubiquity of what we call "T Talk," it can be hard even to recognize them. A jumble of science and folklore, T Talk directs attention away from the most important consequences of the regulations by doing what it does best: making challenges to "common sense" thinking about T and gender seem antiscience. Meanwhile, the building criticisms of the interventions as medically unnecessary intrusions in women's health are, unquestionably, based on science.

The unwanted manipulations of women athletes' bodily integrity also contravene both international human rights law and medical ethics. At the end of May, Semenya filed an appeal to the Federal Supreme Court of Switzerland saying, "I am a woman and I am a world-class athlete. The IAAF will not drug me or stop me from being who I am."

About the Authors

Rebecca M. Jordan-Young is a professor of women's, gender, and sexuality studies at Barnard College. She is the co-author, with Katrina Karkazis, of Testosterone: An Unauthorized Biography *(Harvard University Press, 2019).*

Katrina Karkazis is the Carol Zicklin Chair in the Honors Academy at Brooklyn College and a Senior Visiting Fellow in the Global Health Justice Partnership at Yale University. She is the co-author, with Rebecca M. Jordan-Young, of Testosterone: An Unauthorized Biography *(Harvard University Press, 2019).*

Head Injury and Chronic Brain Damage: It's Complicated

By Brian Levine and Carrie Esopenko

There are two ways to go about studying a disease. Let's call them the retrospective and prospective methods. In the retrospective method, scientists identify individuals with the disease and ask about the circumstances that led to the illness. In the prospective method, they start with a representative sample of people and track them over time to see who develops the disease.

Both methods have yielded important discoveries, but the retrospective method is much more prone to distortion than the prospective method. Consider the following example. Using the retrospective method, 100 percent of alcoholics drink alcohol. Yet drinking alcohol does not necessarily lead to alcoholism, as can be determined by the prospective method in which it can be seen that the proportion of those who enjoy alcoholic drinks and become alcoholics is less than 100 percent.

Boston University's Chronic Traumatic Encephalopathy (CTE) Center recently reported that 99 percent of NFL alumni who made brain donations at the time of death have CTE (a similar finding was reported in 2013). While researchers acknowledge that those who make brain donations are not representative of retired NFL players (much less those with sports-related concussions in general) it is remarkably easy to make the same mistake as in the alcoholism example—that is, making the assumption that this finding generalizes to the broader population of athletes exposed to concussion.

CTE is a neurodegenerative disease initially termed "dementia pugilistica" in boxers by Dr. Harrison Stanford Martland in 1928. It is characterized by changes in mood and cognition but can only be diagnosed through the examination of brain tissue at death. The neuropathologist Bennet Omalu found the same neuropathology in a professional football player in 2005, giving inspiration to the movie *Concussion*.

The seriousness of CTE in those affected is not in doubt. Yet the broader context of CTE research, and its implications for our health and that of our loved ones, has been lacking. CTE has been identified in a few hundred individuals, nearly all of them athletes exposed to hundreds, if not thousands, of impacts to the head. The alarming case studies of suicide or premature death in people with CTE have led many to fear that disability or even death due to CTE is inevitable in those who have suffered concussions. Yet professional football players enjoy a longer lifespan than the average person with risk of suicide half that of the general population.

Mental changes in retired professional athletes are far more complicated than a binary classification of positive or negative for CTE. Many of those with CTE have complicated brain pathology reflecting multiple neurodegenerative conditions. Ex-professional athletes face numerous challenges, including psychiatric conditions and chronic pain overlaid on a unique profile of skills and personality characteristics that presumably attracted them to high level sports competition in the first place. Moreover, the number of people with CTE pathology in their brains who have no outward symptoms is unknown. In fact, it is not unusual for neuropathology of other types, such as Alzheimer's disease, to be found in people who did not show signs of dementia.

At Baycrest's Rotman Research Institute in Toronto, we have been fortunate to interview, test and scan the brains of more than 50 National Hockey League (NHL) alumni in our research on the remote effects of concussion. We found no evidence of cognitive impairment, yet there was an elevated rate of psychological problems, such as depression, anxiety and substance abuse.

While CTE cannot be ruled out, these conditions, which are commonly observed in the absence of concussion history, are treatable. Given media accounts of CTE, many alumni are frightened and wonder if they are on a path towards inexorable decline. Ex-NHLer Todd Ewan, for example, (not a participant in our study) took his life after struggling with depression. His family was convinced that he had CTE, but there was no evidence of this upon neuropathological examination.*

Research on brain changes including CTE in retired professional athletes may lead to important new discoveries about brain trauma, aging and neurodegenerative disease. Although we regard CTE as a legitimate concern for professional athletes with major concussion exposure, is there similar concern warranted for recreational contact sports? Out of the millions exposed to concussions through recreational sports, the count of confirmed cases of CTE in the research literature is in the tens. Yet not even Dr. Omalu is immune to the reasoning error defined above, stating that "there is a 100 percent risk of exposure to permanent brain damage" in those participating in recreational contact sports, and that youth football is a form of child abuse.

Many sports carry risks of injuries that should be managed. On the other hand, lack of exercise and overly sedentary behavior contribute to numerous negative health outcomes. Participation in recreational sports, including contact sports, has many benefits to health and social functioning. Long before the latest wave of research on CTE, it was well known that concussions can be associated with significant functional impairment for weeks following the injury. They also increase the risk of subsequent concussions, where symptoms can be potentiated by prior concussion, especially if full recovery has not occurred.

If you or someone close to you has had a concussion, medical attention is warranted. Avoid activities that could result in another concussion; multiple concussions are associated with poorer recovery. If there are mental changes or psychological distress, seek help. None of these recommendations is altered by the present state of knowledge about CTE, which is in its infancy.

Author's note: Since this article was published, a separate analysis of Mr. Ewan's brain tissue did find evidence of CTE.

About the Author

Brian Levine is a senior scientist at Baycrest's Rotman Research Institute in Toronto and a professor of psychology and medicine (neurology) at the University of Toronto. He is a lead investigator on the Baycrest Brain Health in Professional Athletes Study, involving brain and behavior studies of retired professional ice hockey players.

Olympic Gold May Depend on the Brain's Reward Chemical

By Robin Wylie

Scientists have been searching for a genetic explanation for athletic ability for decades. So far their efforts have focused largely on genes related to physical attributes, such as muscular function and aerobic efficiency. But geneticists have also started to investigate the neurological basis behind what makes someone excel in sports—and new findings implicate dopamine, a neurotransmitter responsible for the feelings of reward and pleasure. Dopamine is also involved in a host of other mental functions, including the ability to deal with stress and endure pain. Consequently, the new research supports the idea that the mental—not just the physical—is what sets elite athletes above the rest.

In an effort to piece together what makes a great athlete great, researchers at the University of Parma in Italy collected DNA from 50 elite athletes (ones who had achieved top scores at an Olympic Games or other international competition) and 100 nonprofessional athletes (ones who played sports regularly, but below competitive level). They then compared four genes across the two groups that had previously been suggested as linked to athletic ability: one related to muscle development, one involved with transporting dopamine in the brain, another that regulates levels of cerebral serotonin and one involved in breaking down neurotransmitters.

The researchers found a significant genetic difference between the two groups in only one of the genes: the one involved in transporting dopamine. Two particular variants of this gene (called the dopamine active transporter, or *DAT*) were significantly more common among the elite athletes than in the control group. One variant was almost five times more prevalent in the elite group (occurring in 24 percent of the elites versus 5 percent of the rest); the other variant was approximately 1.7 times more prevalent

(51 percent versus 30 percent). The results were published in *Journal of Biosciences*.

The idea that dopamine could play a role in mediating athletic ability makes sense, given previous research on the neurotransmitter and *DAT* in particular, says John Salamone, a professor of psychology at the University of Connecticut who was not involved in the research. "Animal studies show that the *DAT* gene is involved with increased motor activity, energy expenditure and reward-seeking behavior," he explains. "So it's plausible that variants of the *DAT* gene could be related to aspects of athletic performance."

Similarly, two studies conducted in 2012 found evidence that genes related to dopamine were associated with increased levels of "risk-seeking" behavior in groups of several hundred skiers and snowboarders. Such behavior could make the difference in which athletes grab the gold, says Cynthia Thomson, a geneticist and sports psychologist at University of the Fraser Valley in British Columbia, who led the studies. "To reach the podium an athlete has to take risks, whether by attempting a more difficult skill to obtain more points or by veering on the edge of control to attain greater speeds," she says. "Our results suggest that variations in the brain's dopamine pathway can affect a person's propensity to take such risks, which could therefore make them more likely to reach elite levels in sport."

Nevertheless, more research will be needed to verify the connection between dopamine and athletic ability—and more still to test whether it is a cause and effect relationship. The dopamine transporter is also behind several disorders such as depression, attention deficit hyperactivity disorder (ADHD), bipolar disorder and Parkinson's disease.

Go Figure: Why Olympic Ice Skaters Don't Fall Flat on Their Faces

By Yasemin Saplakoglu

Watching a fellow human jump into the air, spin three times and land on a thin piece of steel—all the while balancing on slippery ice—is an awe-inspiring experience.

Figure skaters execute their routines so elegantly, they make it look easy—an illusion that quickly dissolves with our own trepid first step in an ice rink. Clinging to the side walls for dear life, feet stinging from the awkward display of ice walking, first-time ice skaters can barely skate in a straight line, let alone balance on one foot. Although it may seem Olympic figure skaters have befriended the ice gods and coaxed the laws of physics to work in their favor, what they have really done is rewire their brains to suppress their reflexes.

If one tilts one's head backward far enough, the body's reflexes will kick in. Neurons that are responsible for firing when the brain senses the body is off-balance will set off a cascade of signals from the inner ear to the brain stem, then to the spinal cord and finally to the muscles that tell the body to lurch forward for the save. In sports like figure skating, the body is frequently in such unlikely positions. So how do skaters convince their brains that it's totally okay the body is halfway to a face-plant?

According to researchers, practice can lead to new maps of neurons in the cerebellum, an area in the back of the brain. So when the skater moves into a position anticipated by the cerebellum, it fires neurons to cancel out reflex signals that would interfere with the desired movement. If someone is slipping on ice and someone else is deliberately jumping, "they might be moving through the world in exactly the same way," says Kathleen Cullen, a neuroscientist at Johns Hopkins University who in 2015 showed this brain mechanism in an experiment with monkeys. In one case, you want your reflexes to work; in the other, you don't. The brain learns to quell reflexes when there's a match between what it expects and what actually happens, she says.

Skaters are also masters at avoiding dizziness. Here again, their brains have learned to subdue a reflex—this time in the eyes. As we move about the world, our eyes automatically move to compensate for slight head movements so we can stare at the same point in space. Normally, if we spin around in an office chair and suddenly stop, we feel like we're still moving. That's because fluid in the inner ear responsible for detecting movement continues to whirl around due to inertia, making your brain think it's still in motion. Because your eyes continue moving to correct your view, you feel dizzy. According to Cullen, what a skater's brain learns to do—through a similar mechanism in the cerebellum—is to ignore the false sense of motion at the end of a spin and greatly reduce that eye reflex.

Training the brain takes time, and that's why "it's only practice that makes perfect," says Rui Costa, a neuroscientist at Columbia University's Zuckerman Institute who also studies the neuroscience of movement. When you look at how seamless most of these routines are, he says, "I mean, it's just amazing." For proof that the brain is continuously working and calibrating itself to help the body adapt to new motions and environments, just step out of the rink after some time skating. The ground will feel weird, as if your brain expects it to be made of ice.

About the Author

Yasemin Saplakoglu is a staff writer at Live Science, covering health, neuroscience, and biology. Her work has appeared in Scientific American, Science and the San Jose Mercury News. She has a bachelor's degree in biomedical engineering from the University of Connecticut and a graduate certificate in science communication from the University of California, Santa Cruz.

The Olympic Motto, Cellular Memories, and the Epigenetic Effects of Doping

By E. Paul Zehr

itius, altius, fortius. Faster, higher, stronger. The modern Olympic motto was proposed by Pierre de Coubertin when the International Olympic Committee was formed way back in 1894. It's meant to capture the essence of competition in sport but is also a signal for many to try and exceed human biological limits by using external enhancements in the form of "doping." A very well-known example of doping in sport is the use of androgenic steroids. What people outside of strength-training circles don't necessarily know, however, is that substances like steroids can still have an effect after athletes stop using them.

Even without steroids, someone who has trained extensively and then stopped reacquires muscle mass and strength more rapidly than someone who hadn't trained at all. This was thought to be due to rapid changes in the nervous system affecting the coordination and activation of the muscles, which might in turn relate to what scientists call "epigenetics."

There was much excitement when the human genome was first sequenced a decade and a half ago, but the latest hot topic—and one with significant impact for doping, suspension, and possible return to play—is the epigenome. The epigenome determines which genes actually get activated and expressed by what kind of cells, and when. If the genome contains the essence of your genetic potential, epigenetics is the way your potential—all your ability for faster, higher, stronger—is brought forward and used. The genome is like a dictionary full of words, most of which aren't all used at once—and some of which are never used at all. Epigenetics is the process of pulling those words out and usefully applying them in sentences for the conversations you need to have. Epigenetics essentially bridges the gap between nature and nurture.

More specifically, it describes how gene expression is regulated and what genes are expressed in an organism. This does not change the actual nucleotide sequences—the building blocks—in the genes. The epigenetic changes that happen to you in the course of your life affect the next generation of cells that you produce.

While every cell in your body carries your genome, your epigenome has a number of flavors, depending upon the cell and tissue type. The key things about epigenetics are that it affects gene expression, changes during development (when stem cells are differentiating into the cells they are going to become), and changes in disease states.

Cancer, of all diseases, has been the one linked most clearly with epigenetic changes. For example, a gene that when activated produces lung cancer might only be expressed and activated when an environmental cue is present, like cigarette smoke. But biology isn't typically that simple: linking diseases directly to DNA changes is difficult. This is largely because changes that yield disorders often occur outside the parts of the DNA that code for proteins and that we understand better.

This is where biologist Ingrid Egner and her colleagues in Norway enter the story. They were interested in the effect of training on muscle growth. Unlike most other cell types, muscle fibers have multiple nuclei. During strength training, muscle mass increases, and the number of nuclei in each cell also goes up. This team wanted to know if this "cellular memory mechanism" could be influenced by steroids. They gave mice a testosterone derivative for 14 days, which produced about a 66 percent increase in nuclei and a 77 percent increase in the size of the muscle fibers. Three weeks after withdrawing testosterone, the size of the muscle fibers had reverted to the level found in animals that had never trained or been given drugs.

This part of the experiment was to cause a change in the "memory" within the nuclei of the muscle fibers. While the size of the fibers fluctuated, the number of nuclei remained elevated for three months after the testosterone was withdrawn. Did this mean that the muscle fibers would respond differently to training? That is, would they respond like "normal" or enhanced muscle because of the larger number of nuclei?

In the next part of the experiment, two groups of animals (the ones who were previously exposed to the testosterone derivative and the "control" animals that weren't) were strength-trained for six days. Control mice failed to show any appreciable increase in muscle fiber size after this short period, while, in contrast, the testosterone-exposed mice showed a 31 percent increase.

Previously untrained muscle fibers recruit nuclei from activated satellite (stem) cells before growing larger. The nuclei are the command centers driving the muscle cells to produce more protein to get larger and stronger, and it seems that this greater number of nuclei is retained and protected over time. Muscle fibers with this higher number of nuclei then grow faster when given an exercise stress like strength training. This "memory" of prior strength apparently remains stable for up to 15 years and may be permanent.

The relevance for doping in sport is that even a brief period of anabolic steroid use may cause long-lasting performance enhancements that continue many years after use is discontinued. It is almost as if the "use it or lose it" adage has been changed to "depending upon what you used you might not really ever lose it." We don't know for sure how this may relate to other performance enhancing drugs. But if an athlete takes something to enhance her abilities very quickly and then stops, she may forever possess the enhanced ability to be retrained quickly.

In real life where there are no rules on competition, this is a great example of the plasticity of physiology. In sport it's a great example of how *citius, altius, fortius* can be achieved in ways that circumvent the rules of competition.

About the Author

E. Paul Zehr is a professor of neuroscience and kinesiology at the University of Victoria in British Columbia. His research focuses on the neural control of arm and leg movement during gait and recovery of walking after neurotrauma. His recent popular science books include Becoming Batman: The Possibility of a Superhero *(Johns Hopkins University Press, 2008),* Inventing Iron Man: The Possibility of a Human Machine *(Johns Hopkins University Press, 2011),* Project Superhero *(ECW Press, 2014), and* Chasing Captain America: How Advances in Science, Engineering and Biotechnology Will Produce a Superhuman *(ECW Press, 2018). He is also a regular speaker at San Diego International Comic-Con, New York Comic-Con, and Wonder Con. He has a popular neuroscience blog, Black Belt Brain, at* Psychology Today.

Are We Reaching the End of World Records?

By Karl J. P. Smith

In 1896 Charilaos Vasilakos won the first modern marathon, a qualifying race for Greece's Olympic team, with a time of three hours and eighteen minutes. Today that would not even qualify him for the Boston Marathon. Since the beginning of the modern Olympic Games world records in every sport have advanced sharply, driven by factors as disparate as global conflicts, social change, technological improvements and changing rules.

The general upward trend in performance is largely due to advances in our understanding of fitness, conditioning, diet and nutrition, says Mark Williams, a professor of sport, health and exercise science at Brunel University in London.

But this progress has not been steady, and many things have helped or hindered it. As an example, Geoffroy Berthelot of the National Institute of Sport and Physical Education (INSEP) in Paris highlights the stagnation of most records during World War I and World War II. "When you have world wars you don't focus on sport competition," Berthelot says. But conversely, the cold war led to the Soviet Union and its satellites developing a rigorous scientific approach to athlete improvement—an aggressive illegal doping program notwithstanding. Some event records set during that time have never been beaten, such as the Men's Hammer Throw world record, which was last broken by Soviet hammer thrower Yuri Sedykh in 1986 at the European Championships in Stuttgart, three years before the fall of the Berlin Wall and five years before the U.S.S.R. collapsed. "Today we have a lot of difficulty [with breaking the records] because athletes use less doping substances," Berthelot says.

Social change can also drive performance, as it seems to have done in women's marathon times. Women were excluded from performing in many such events, including the Boston Marathon, because it was commonly believed their constitutions could not handle long races. In 1966 Roberta Gibb hid in the bushes beside the starting line of the Marathon and became the first known woman to complete the course. The next year Kathrine Switzer entered the race under the name K. V. Switzer, and photos of the race organizers trying (unsuccessfully) to remove her forcefully mid-race made international headlines. These events coincided with Second-Wave feminism in the U.S., and a dedicated campaign brought the Women's Marathon to the 1984 Summer Olympics held in Los Angeles.

Technical breakthroughs have also played a role, as illustrated by the evolution of the high jump. At the 1968 Olympics in Mexico City, U.S. Olympian Dick Fosbury shocked the world with an innovative technique called the Fosbury flop, in which he turned his back to the bar when he jumped, rather than cross it face down. Fosbury won the gold medal that year but did not break the world record. It would take several years for athletes to do so using the technique, which would ultimately enable dramatically higher jumps. That kind of advancement is not uncommon, says Jordan Taylor, a psychologist at Princeton University who studies skill acquisition. "What happens is that you basically get a little bit of a slowdown until someone comes up with a new strategy—and then when you have a new strategy, it takes a little bit of time to refine it, and then you see the progression go on," Taylor says.

The pace of world record–breaking has slowed, as humans reach physiological limits and the International Association of Athletics Federations cracks down on doping. Berthelot is an author on two papers that suggest the rate of world record–breaking peaked in 1988. There are some exceptions to the general slowdown that has followed. One is swimming, but Berthelot calls this progress a "technological artifact" that came from the brief adoption of polyurethane swimsuits in 2008–09—and his paper suggests that, in swimming at least, we should get used to the records we have.

About the Author

Karl J. P. Smith is an AAAS Mass Media Fellow and current Ph.D. candidate in biophysics, computation, and structural biology at the University of Rochester. He is the typewriting storyteller behind 10 Cent Stories and is the co-creator of the Bench Warmer's Podcast.

Section 2: The Psychology of Sports

Home Advantage Doesn't Require Crowds, COVID Pro Soccer Matches Show

By Diana Kwon

B efore COVID-19 halted public life as we know it, professional soccer matches drew in enormous crowds. In stadiums filled with tens of thousands of people, a chorus of cheers, jeers, boos and moans would follow the ball, zigzagging from one player to another, as both teams tried to score. But in pandemic times, these games stay eerily quiet. The roaring masses are gone, and in their place, ghostly rows of empty seats remain.

This unprecedented circumstance has provided researchers with a unique opportunity to study the effect of spectators on the so-called home advantage—a well-documented phenomenon in which sports teams stand a greater chance of winning when playing in their own stadium. Support from home fans, who make up a large proportion of the crowd, has long been thought to contribute to this effect by motivating players and influencing referees' decisions.

The benefit that fans bring is not the only explanation for the boon that accrues to home teams. It could also come from the effects of travel on the visiting opponents, the local teams' familiarity with the venue or territoriality—a defensive response to the invasion of one's home. Territoriality is commonly seen in animals, but researchers have found that soccer players' testosterone levels rise more before home games than away ones, suggesting the phenomenon may also play a role in sports.

Determining the degree of these factors' influence persists as a challenge because it is difficult to test their effects experimentally, says Daniel Memmert, a sports scientist at the German Sport University Cologne. He and his colleagues decided to take advantage of the opportunity to undertake a natural social science experiment—a large stretch of audience-free matches afforded by the pandemic—to assess how much the presence of fans influenced the outcomes of games.

The researchers examined matches played by 10 professional soccer leagues across six countries: Spain, England, Italy, Germany, Portugal and Turkey. They compared the outcomes of more than 36,000 games played under normal circumstances—from the 2010–2011 season to the start of the pandemic in the 2019–2020 season—with those from 1,006 games played without onlookers in 2020.

The analysis, published today in *PLOS ONE*, reveals a small but statistically insignificant drop in the home advantage. Prior to the pandemic, on average, the proportion of wins, draws and losses was 45, 27 and 28 percent, respectively. During the pandemic, without fans to fill the stadium, home teams won 43 percent of the time, drew 25 percent of the time and lost 32 percent of the time. When the researchers looked more closely at the data, they found that while there appeared to only be a minute effect on outcome, there were significant impacts on other aspects of the game. In the absence of spectators, referees were less likely to penalize the visiting teams—for example, by giving out yellow or red cards—and the home teams had less match dominance (as measured by the number of direct attempts to score a goal). "We found that spectators do not have a direct influence on the outcome of a match, but what is happening on the pitch is different," Memmert says.

At this point, why spectators' influences on referee behavior and match dominance did not have a significant impact on the outcomes of games is an open question. Overall, however, the results of this study suggest that factors such as familiarity and territoriality may be playing a bigger role than spectator support, Memmert says.

Dane McCarrick, a sports psychology researcher at the University of Leeds in England and a professional soccer referee, says that while the study is noteworthy, one of its potential limitations is the inclusion of all games since 2010—a lengthy stretch that needs to take into account variables such as changes in players, where games were played and rules. For example, the video assistant referee (VAR), a tool that enables referees to review incidents before making decisions, has only been introduced over the past few years. In a preprint study recently posted on PsyArXiv, McCarrick and his colleagues also examined the effect of the pandemic on games played by 15 European soccer leagues during the 2019–2020 season—and came to a different conclusion. They found that the chances of a home team win decreased during spectatorless matches.

Sandy Wolfson, a sports and exercise psychologist at Northumbria University in England and a co-author of McCarrick's study, notes that several groups have been looking at the empty stadiums' effects on the home advantage. "Most of the studies I've looked at have suggested that the home advantage has been decreased since COVID, but it's there," she says, "which suggests that there are other factors at work that need to be considered." Being able to conduct these studies has been "the only perk of this horrible pandemic, because prior to COVID, you'd never be able to convince the team to not allow their fans in," Wolfson says. "It worked really well to our advantage."

About the Author

Diana Kwon is a freelance journalist who covers health and the life sciences. She is based in Berlin.

How Overtraining Can Trap Athletes

By Sarah Tuff Dunn

Two years after breaking my leg in a freak running accident, I was logging up to 100 miles a week on the treadmill in preparation for a 36-hour adventure race. A veteran of 15 marathons and countless other athletic events, I was in peak physical shape. Or so I thought—until one Sunday morning when I could barely lift my arms. After years of lifting weights, I was too tired to lift the laundry basket. My own fitness, it seemed, had felled me. Was it overtraining? Had I pushed so far beyond my limits that my body could no longer keep up?

"Anyone who does endurance sports plays with the concept of overreaching," says Jeffrey B. Kreher, a sports medicine specialist at Massachusetts General Hospital. "But overtraining is when the ability to tolerate stress is greatly diminished for whatever reason. The homeostasis of the body has reached its tipping point." Kreher and fellow physician Jennifer Schwartz, now at Beth Israel Deaconess Medical Center, published a comprehensive review of the condition—"Overtraining Syndrome: A Practical Guide"—in 2012 in *Sports Health*.

In practice, overtraining can be hard to diagnose. Among the first signs are performance plateaus or declines. Resting heart rates can shift either up or down. Extreme fatigue and sore muscles set in. Ultimately overtraining disrupts the delicate balance of multiple systems, throwing off hormones, the immune system, behavior and mood. These effects can cause a confusingly broad range of possible symptoms—insomnia, irritability, anxiety, weight loss, anorexia, a loss of motivation, a lack of concentration and depression.

No one knows what biological mechanism triggers the syndrome. One theory holds that it is caused by a breakdown of the hypothalamus, a brain structure that regulates many hormones, metabolic functions and the autonomic nervous system. "It's confounding," Kreher says. "It's a retrospective diagnosis, and fatigue doesn't mean you have overtraining syndrome. Not all depression is overtraining. An individual's stress tolerance has many different influences."

As Kreher and Schwartz point out in their review, trouble tends to begin when additional stressors appear in an athlete's life. "It might be excessive travel, it might be the pressure of the competition season, it might be monotony," Kreher explains, illuminating one reason why my own endless treadmill miles had left me at a dead end. He notes that Olympic athletes, who are under tremendous pressure, can be especially vulnerable to overtraining. Some experts estimate that about 60 percent of elite runners and about 30 percent of elite swimmers overtrain at some point during their career.

It is something long-distance runner and former Olympian Ryan Hall knows all too well. Once a favorite for this summer's Olympic Games, he withdrew in January because of extreme fatigue, following in the exhausted footsteps of famed triathletes Paula Newby-Fraser and Scott Tinley. When Hall called it quits, it was the end of a two-year battle with underperformance. Was it overtraining? Like me, he is not sure but comments: "If you want to run 2:04 for a marathon, you're going to have to train very, very long and intensely, and at some point that demand on your body will take its toll." For Hall, the toll was mostly physical. "If I tried to run," he says, "I felt like I weighed a million pounds and could hardly lift my legs." For others, though, the distress is mainly mental.

The best treatment for overtraining is rest—which may sound easy: just snooze on the couch until your strength returns. But that prescription presents a challenge to athletes who have been conditioned for decades to train and compete. For elite athletes such as Hall, Kreher adds, it also raises an existential question of "Now what?" After cutting his running to three days a week, 30 minutes a session, and adding weight training to his routine, Hall is once again enjoying his sport, although he has retired from elite events. "My energy feels better than it felt my entire running career," he reports. "It's a bummer not to be going to Rio, but I'm choosing to be grateful for the two Olympics I did get to go to."

There are no evidence-based ways to prevent overtraining, Kreher says, but adding miles gradually and learning to be more resilient to stress—along with getting enough calories, hydration, sleep and carbohydrates—are key fitness fundamentals. Focusing on feelings can also help keep energy levels up. By recording their postworkout moods, for example, collegiate swimmers in a multicounty study reduced burnout by 10 percent, Kreher says. "If you do physical activity and feel joy, rejuvenation and health afterward, then that's appropriate," he concludes. "If you feel it was work, then that's a sign to do something different."

I've been following that sage advice myself lately, and after a long period of exhaustion, I am back running again.

About the Author

Sarah Tuff Dunn, an avid runner, has written for the New York Times, National Geographic Adventure, Forbes, *and* Time, *among other publications.*

Sports Psychologists Extend Their Counseling to Athletes' Coaches and Families

By Katherine Harmon

T he crowd has quieted, but an electric energy from the packed grandstands fills the air. The diver stands atop the platform, aware of television cameras below that are broadcasting his every muscle twitch to millions of viewers worldwide. He can smell the chlorine wafting up from the diving pool 10 meters below. The texture of the platform feels rough beneath his feet. He takes a breath, makes his approach and jumps sharply upward. Then he twists through the air, executing a perfect dive and, finally, with no more than a few drops of splash, knifes smoothly into the cool water.

The diver opens his eyes. Feeling confident and relaxed, he now looks ahead at the platform and gets ready to climb the familiar ladder to make his practice dive before the actual competition, still weeks down the road.

This diver had just gone through one of his most important workouts before he actually stands up on the Olympic diving platform: visualization. Olympic divers, such as David Boudia and Thomas Finchum, as well as other top athletes, use trusted psychological tactics such as visualization and positive self-talk to stay at the top of their games—even when the pressure is on. Yet the sports psychologists who teach these techniques now have more scientific results in hand, and they are learning that the athlete's mental tools are just the jumping-off point to achieving peerless performance. Giving an athlete or team the best chance of bringing home the gold also requires creating an entire environment of carefully constructed group and interpersonal dynamics. Sports psychologists are no longer just training athletes. They are also training the coaches and family members in the competitors' lives.

"We've learned a lot in the past 10 or 15 years about how to be more effective" in teaching everyone around an athlete how to help him or her excel, says Daniel Gould, professor of applied sports psychology at Michigan State University. And the athletes say the work is paying off.

Getting Inside the Coach's Head

Even an athlete in the most individual of sports is part of a complex network of relationships. Coach, family, friends, even team administrators are an extensive and often under-recognized part of the experience. Elite athletes might be better than the average person at shutting out distractions, managing their emotions and controlling their energy levels. But they are not immune to an overbearing parent, negative coach or unsupportive teammate.

Coaches and support staff, whether they realize it or not, are creating a mental environment for athletes, not just a physical training regimen. And although sports psychologists are often deployed for the benefit of the athletes, "a lot of times we work through the coach because the coach is creating a psychological climate," Gould says.

Counselors are achieving "a huge gain in better educating our coaches," Gould continues. By the time an athlete reaches college or professional levels, coaches are almost operating like CEOs, Gould notes. They're in charge of coordinating a huge organization of specialists—athletes, nutritionists, strength coaches, media liaisons and psychologists. So to gain access to athletes, physically and mentally, a sports psychologist must first be accepted and supported by the coach. Then the expert can start working to help the coach maintain a productive, balanced emotional arena for the athletes. Gould describes this environment as a fine balance of autonomy— individually empowered athletes and staff—and connectivity, essentially a feeling of relatedness among the entire group. "That's pretty easy to say," Gould says. But helping coaches and teams achieve that state is no small task. Especially when everyone is under extreme stress of high-level competition.

At professional or Olympic levels, coaches are increasingly in the spotlight. "Their job is in many ways harder than the athlete's," Gould says. "They're trying to create an environment for the athletes, and at the same time the coach gets nervous, so sometimes they overcoach." Combine that with nervous athletes and tensions can rise, hampering an athlete's ability to perform at his or her best.

For team sports, of course, creating cohesion and good communication among team members—whether for synchronized swimming, volleyball, doubles tennis or even equestrian events—is key. To excel, players also need to feel confident about their own roles as well as their contributions to the team, notes Craig Wrisberg, a professor emeritus of sport psychology and past president of the Association for Applied Sport Psychology (AASP).

Family Gain or Drain?

Athletes also have people outside of the sport's circle in their daily lives. Friends and family members can provide mental stability, but they can also be a psychological drain. Even for veteran athletes, "one of their greatest supports is their family—and it's also one of their biggest distractions," says Chris Carr, a sport and performance psychologist at Indiana University Bloomington, who has coached previous Olympic teams, including the 2008 U.S. Olympic diving team. Carr had learned this over years of working and talking with athletes. Long before the team left for Beijing, he and his colleagues held workshops for divers' family and friends to teach *them* how they could provide the most support—and the least distraction.

Other psychologists have focused their efforts on helping athletes smooth over these support relationships themselves. Adeline Gray, a 2012 Olympic hopeful as an alternate for the first U.S. women's wrestling team, can attest to the powerful role sports psychology can play in helping her support network help her. Gray knows that to do her best she needs to be calm and upbeat before hitting the mat. "If I get too jittery, it's too much," she says.

But her father, who has been one of her biggest supporters and long-time coach, had a habit of trying to pump her up before matches, getting in her face and yelling. This interference was starting to get to Gray. So her sports psychologist helped her work up the courage to ask her dad, instead, for a hug and a smile. Just like that, her dad switched to the hug, and she was able to enter into her matches in a better frame of mind.

Gray, who is 21, has been working with a sports psychologist since she was in her mid-teens. She says she encourages other athletes to find one to meet with—even if they just chat about their dog, she says. "It's one more thing that's going smoothly in your life so you can focus on your sport."

Always an Individual Sport

Psychologists are focusing more on their own relationship with an athlete, too. Mental preparation is likely to be very different for a weight lifter, who needs an explosive burst of almost superhuman energy and strength, than it is for a marksman, who must calm her mind and even her heart rate while aiming. Understanding an individual's personality and habits will improve how well the sports psychologist can best help the athlete.

Carr prepared the U.S. Olympic diving team for the 2008 summer Olympics in Beijing. By the time the opening ceremonies launched, "I had worked with a number of those athletes for four years— through observations and one-on-one discussions," he says. Benefits accrued not just from his formal sessions with athletes or the team, he says, but casual, incidental interactions, such as "the informal bus ride chat from the training facility to the Olympic Village," where he could check in and see how athletes were feeling and make sure they had their mental checklists ready to go.

After that much time, Carr was intimately acquainted with the concentration, confidence or composure challenges each diver faced. So when it came time for them to prepare for their big days, he had constructed a "very tailor-made intervention" for each athlete"—important, he notes, because "the Olympics is different than everything else."

Despite his years of experience with U.S. Olympic teams, Carr says that if he got a call tomorrow to help out with the 2012 team he would think twice about it, fearing that not having been there all along could make him more of a detriment and distraction than an asset. Gray agrees that history is key in relationships between athletes and their sports psychologists. After her psychologist of a few years changed positions Gray started working with someone new. It was tough, Gray says, to form a new relationship with someone lacking the history and deep knowledge of her previous challenges and successes that her former psychologist had.

On the other hand, Gray notes, the athlete must be willing to develop the relationship. "It does take time and commitment," she says. "And it's a two-way street; it's hard to release your emotions and allow someone into your personal life and tell them I do *this* before a competition and not worry they'll think you're crazy."

Nevertheless, a coach has even more history with an athlete, and it falls to coaches to implement a lot of the mental training. The key is to push athletes beyond their mental comfort levels, allowing them to fail sometimes, but not to break them, Gould says. This can build mental toughness seen in many elite athletes, but for coaches to do this successfully takes skill and individual knowledge.

Special mental preparation is needed to soar at the lofty Olympics. "It's a lot of emotion, it's a lot of energy, it's a lot of pieces," Carr says. And "If you fall short of your goals, how do you manage that?" Sure enough, sports psychologists have further broadened their scope by helping athletes *after* their event. A team loss in a close soccer game might be tough, but how does a psychologist help a diver or a gymnast regain composure after a single mistake that they know could have just cost them a medal? That's where the mental toughness training comes in, AASP's Wrisberg says. "Mentally tough athletes are really good at making adjustments and doing them quickly. They look for a lesson in it, and if there's none, they move on," he says. "Otherwise, it's a downward spiral, and it gets pretty ugly."

Taking Training to the Next Level

Widening sports psychology beyond individual athlete training still involves a lot of trial and error. Despite a wealth of scientific papers being published on everything from parents of young tennis players to competitive college teams, studies of truly elite athletes are relatively few and far between. That leaves most sports psychologists to craft their own approaches, rather than work from an industry standard. "We have to use the artistic nature of our profession," Carr says.

The field is spotty on a global scale. Although many pro and Olympic—and even college—teams in the U.S. and other wealthier countries work extensively with sports psychologists, most teams across the world do not have this luxury. One of the biggest challenges facing the field, however, is that it's nearly impossible to measure results. Athletes can report what they were thinking and how they felt, and those answers can be measured against the competitive results. But Gould says that's not good enough. Brain-imaging studies are likely to be the next step in improving the mental game. With a peek into high-performers' brain activity, sports psychology and coaches might be able to learn some of the secrets to success—and then try to teach these ways of thinking to other athletes.

Not even the best mental preparation can guarantee gold. But, says Carr, it can help an athlete "be able to compete when their Olympic moment comes."

The Not-So-Hot Hand

By John Matson

Reggie Miller, Michael Jordan, Kobe Bryant. They've all gone on seemingly memorable shooting streaks. But past research has shown that the so-called hot hand is a myth, rooted in our tendency to see patterns where there are none.

Myth or no, the shooters still seem to think they're on fire when statistics show they're not. A recent study finds that professional basketball players put too much stock in the outcome of their last three-point shot. If they make a three-pointer, they are much more likely to try another one than if they had missed. The study, appearing in the journal *Nature Communications*, used game stats for hundreds of NBA and WNBA players. (*Scientific American* is part of Nature Publishing Group.)

The Lakers' Bryant was a prime example in his MVP season of 2007–2008. When Bryant made a three-pointer, he shot again from downtown nearly four times as often as he did following a missed three. But trying to ride a three-point streak is often bad strategy. Players actually tend to shoot a lower percentage after making shots than after missing them—once again sending the idea of the "hot hand" up in smoke.

About the Author

John Matson is a former reporter and editor for Scientific American *who has written extensively about astronomy and physics.*

Elite Soccer Refs Have Eagle-Eye Ability for Spotting Foul Play

By Catherine Caruso

In the closing seconds of a tied soccer game two opposing players sprint into the penalty box in pursuit of a loose ball and collide, limbs flailing as they both fall to the turf. Instantly, all eyes are on the head referee, tasked with the unenviable job of making a game-changing decision without the benefit of a slow-motion replay. Recent research suggests, however, that elite soccer referees have something working in their favor—enhanced perceptual and cognitive skills that help them make the right call.

In the study, published this week in *Cognitive Research: Principles and Implications*, researchers had elite and sub-elite referees make calls based on video footage of soccer plays while an eye-tracking system recorded where on the screen they were looking. The elite referees were not only better than the amateurs at making the correct call, they were also better at anticipating where the foul would occur before it happened.

As humans, we rely on our perceptual-cognitive skills to navigate the complex events that continuously unfold around us. Any given situation starts with the perceptual—we watch an event as it happens, relying on our eyes to capture what we see and relay it to our brains. Then the cognitive phase begins, as our brains process the information and help us interpret it so we can decide what to do next. Of course, the more intense the situation, the more challenging this becomes—for example, if we are asked to process information and make a decision under pressure. Perhaps unsurprisingly, elite athletes have top-notch perceptual-cognitive skills—they are adept at focusing their attention on the most relevant part of an event and using the information to react accordingly. But what about referees, the oft-overlooked individuals charged with keeping the athletes in line?

Researchers from the University of Leuven in Belgium enrolled 20 elite referees from the two highest-level professional soccer divisions in the country, along with 19 sub-elite referees active at lower competitive levels. The referees watched video clips of foul play situations filmed from a first-person perspective near the action, categorized as either open play situations (where one or two attackers engaged with two defenders) or corner kick situations (where six or seven attackers scrapped with six or seven defenders in front of the goal). Each clip contained one interaction, and referees were asked if a foul had occurred and how they would rate the severity— that is, whether they would assign a yellow or red card. Meanwhile an eye-tracking system consisting of a camera and infrared lights recorded where on the screen the referees were looking to assess how they were focusing their attention. "Eye movements are the mirror of the mind," says Werner Helsen, a kinesiologist and the study's senior author. "Whatever you look at, you pay attention to."

The researchers found that elite referees made the correct call 61 percent of the time, compared with 45 percent for the sub-elite refs. Furthermore, elite referees were better at honing in on the bodily appendages and areas the players would use to commit the foul. "It was clear that the more elite a referee you are, the more you anticipate and the more you look at the specific spots where the foul will be committed," explains Helsen, who adds that less experienced referees were more likely to be looking at the wrong location. For example, the ref might focus on a player's arms although the foul was committed with the offender's legs.

According to Helsen, elite referees do not have an innate talent for making accurate calls—rather, they develop their skills via extensive practice. The key to success for refs then is not only to know where to look but to have the experience to interpret what they see and make a correct decision. "The eyes are useless if the mind is blind," Helsen says.

The next step is finding new and innovative ways to train referees so they can gain experience and improve their perceptual-cognitive skills outside of a game situation, much like the intensive training athletes engage in prior to a competition. Helsen has already developed a Web-based application that referees used to prepare for the 2016 UEFA European Championship in France.

Gershon Tenenbaum, a professor of sport and exercise psychology at The Florida State University who was not involved in the research, praises the study but points out that it was conducted in a laboratory, which means referees did not have to contend with game dynamics such as external pressure from coaches, players and spectators as well as physiological factors such as an elevated heart rate or fatigue. Nevertheless, he adds that the study confirms the findings of previous research on experts in a variety of areas.

Helsen points out that even mundane tasks such as driving require us to use our perceptual-cognitive skills under pressure. And the stakes are much higher for police officers, firefighters, pilots, soldiers or surgeons—where the way they focus their attention and how they interpret information and make decisions can be a matter of life or death. "I see more and more that the way people become experts across disciplines is very, very similar," Helsen says.

Coaching Can Make or Break an Olympic Athlete

By Rachel Nuwer

T hroughout this month the world's top athletes will take to the field, court and pool at the Summer Olympics in Rio de Janeiro. Some, however, will far outshine the others and land numerous medals. Researchers have a special term for these best of the best: superelites.

What differentiates a superelite from someone who competes at the Olympics but goes home empty-handed? New research suggests it can come down to the coach-athlete relationship. According to findings presented in November at the World Class Performance Conference in London, superelites felt that their coaches fully satisfied their emotional needs by acting as friends, mentors and unwavering supporters—in addition to providing superb technical support. High-performing athletes who were not medaled did not feel that way. "This turns on its head a long-held view that we must simply pair the best technical and tactical coaches to our best athletes to achieve ultimate performance," says Matthew Barlow, a postdoctoral researcher in sport psychology at Bangor University in Wales, who led the study.

Barlow and his colleagues were commissioned to find out what it takes to win multiple gold medals by the governmental organization UK Sport, which promotes the nation's elite sports and athletic development. The researchers initially identified 43 variables that reliably predicated the probability that someone would become a superelite. One of those factors was the coach-athlete relationship, so UK Sport funded a second in-depth analysis that focused solely on this aspect.

So Barlow and his colleagues recruited 16 male and female superelite athletes, all of whom had won gold at a major championship (such as the Olympics). They also recruited 16 athletes who had competed in such championships but never medaled. The groups were matched in sport, age and gender. The scientists then conducted in-depth interviews with the athletes as well as their parents and coaches. After analyzing the results they found that all the athletes said they were technically supported by their coaches—but it was the superelites who reported they also enjoyed thorough emotional support. "Superelite athletes perceived their need for emotional and esteem support were met in a way that the elites did not," Barlow says.

Coaches of superelites acted almost as surrogate parents, praising their athletes' efforts, emphasizing unwavering belief in them, providing positive feedback and taking an interest in personal lives. "A cyclist might come in and the coach says, 'Hey, you're not looking quite right, let's have a coffee and talk about difficulties you might be having at home,'" Barlow says. "They have a bond that goes beyond spreadsheets, power outputs and graphs." Some elite athletes, on the other hand, felt invisible to their coaches or sensed their mentors seemed to expect failure at key moments when they most needed support.

Coaching, of course, isn't the only factor that contributes to an athlete's rise to superelite status. The original study—which is the most comprehensive look at top-performing athletes to date—also revealed significant psychological and life history differences between superstars and their elite counterparts. For example, superelites tended to have experienced a childhood trauma as well as a mid-career turning point). But Barlow and his colleagues still think that the coach-athlete relationship plays a significant role when it comes to shining on the Olympic field.

This study provides evidence for what experts have previously hypothesized about coaching, says Jonathan Fader, a clinical and sport psychologist in New York City who was not involved in the study. The best coaches, he explains, "spend their time using their own playing experience or coaching acumen to help a player build and maintain confidence about the fundamental and unchanging ability that they have. This usually involves a positive, thoughtful and understanding relationship."

Up until now UK Sport has paired athletes and coaches based only on an athlete's ability and a coach's record of success. But the organization is now working with Barlow and his colleagues to design a new method that takes into account the full relationship between the two. UK Sport also hopes to train the competitors to be their own coaches in some ways. "Another challenge we're working on is how to develop self-sufficient athletes," Barlow says. "Being aware of the perceived needs of an athlete—and designing a structure around them—is very different than pandering to their every whim."

About the Author

Rachel Nuwer is a freelance journalist and author of Poached: Inside the Dark World of Wildlife Trafficking *(Da Capo Press, 2018). She lives in Brooklyn, N.Y.*

No One Wins Gold for Practicing the Most

By Karl J. P. Smith

I s it safe to assume that a gold medalist at the Olympics practiced more than a silver medalist—and that a silver medalist practiced more than a bronze winner? Definitely not, according to a new analysis, which looked at nearly 3,000 athletes. The study found that although becoming world class takes an enormous amount of practice, the success of elite athletes cannot be predicted based on the number of hours they spend in careful training.

In 1993 Swedish psychologist K. Anders Ericsson published a highly influential paper that suggested performance differences between mediocre musicians and their superior counterparts—as determined by the evaluations of their professors—were largely determined by the number of hours they spent practicing. He would later publish work extending his theory to other pursuits, including sports, chess and medicine. Ericsson emphasized that there was no upper bound to the effect that deliberate practice had on success in these areas—the world's best athletes, musicians and doctors were simply the ones who practiced the most. His work would eventually be popularized by journalist Malcolm Gladwell and others as the "10,000-hour rule," which suggests that top performance in virtually any field is simply a matter of putting in 10,000 hours of work.

But a new study published in *Perspectives on Psychological Science* shows—as others have—that deliberate practice is just one factor that makes world sports champions. "More or less across the board, practice will improve one's performance," says Brooke Macnamara, a psychologist at Case Western University and lead author of the study. At a certain level of success, however, other factors determine who is the absolute best, she says.

Macnamara and her colleagues analyzed 34 studies that—put together—had tracked the number of hours 2,765 athletes had practiced. Those studies also recorded the athletes' achievements, as determined by either objective measure such as a race time, expert rating of performance or membership in elite groups. For sports at all levels, including athletes performing at a state level or in clubs, deliberate practice could explain 18 percent of the differences in achievement between athletes. But when the researchers looked only at the very best competitors—those who had competed in the Olympics or other world competitions—differences in the number of hours they had practiced explained just 1 percent of the difference in their performance at sporting events. "This suggests that practice is important to a point, but it stops differentiating who's good and who's great," Macnamara says. At the national and global level, a poorly understood mixture of genetics, psychological traits and other factors influence performance.

Ericsson, who is now a professor at The Florida State University, thought that the criteria used in the meta-analysis to define deliberate practice was not strict enough because it grouped self-directed activities and other kinds of practice into the category of deliberate practice, instead of exclusively looking at teacher-directed assignments with immediate feedback. "They have a very different idea of what we're talking about with deliberate practice," he says. Ericsson does acknowledge, however, that the kind of practice he has in mind—in which athletes are closely monitored by coaches at all times—is uncommon in sports. Indeed, applying his new, stricter definition would even exclude some of his own studies on the effect of deliberate practice.

Many in the field see the question of "10,000 hours" as academic rather than practical. "The majority of the scientists in the field would acknowledge that practice is important in the development of expertise, but at the same time I guess that we accept that other factors would contribute," says Mark Williams, a sport, health and exercise scientist at Brunel University London who was not involved in the research. "[The new study] is an interesting paper, but I don't think it's going to necessarily change what people are currently doing," he says.

Jeffrey Fairbrother, a motor behavior scientist at the University of Tennessee who was also not part of the study, agrees that the new research probably will not change how athletes practice: "If we're trying to translate this into usable information for a coach or for an athlete, I don't know how interested they are in us picking each other apart like we do when we're trying to disprove things from a theoretical perspective," he says. "We know that performance can be profoundly influenced by the right training experiences. Shouldn't we focus on providing those experiences to as many people as possible so that they can reach their potential?"

Macnamara says the meta-study opens the way for a more nuanced understanding of the way multiple factors combine and contribute to performance. "I don't know if we'll ever be able to 100 percent explain [what makes an elite athlete], but I think we can do better than what we're doing now."

About the Author

Karl J. P. Smith is an AAAS Mass Media Fellow and current Ph.D. candidate in biophysics, computation, and structural biology at the University of Rochester. He is the typewriting storyteller behind 10 Cent Stories and is the co-creator of the Bench Warmer's Podcast.

Section 3: Sports Technology

Why Baseballs Are Flying in 2019

By Steve Mirsky

An analysis of the 2019 edition of the Major League baseball points to reasons why it's leaving ballparks at a record rate.

Justin Verlander of the Houston Astros will start tonight's Major League Baseball All-Star Game for the American League. He's in the news for more than that, though. Monday, he told ESPN that the huge rise in home runs this season is due to the fact that the 2019 baseball is what he called "a f-ing joke." Many other players and commentators have questioned whether the ball is "juiced"—that is, made so that it travels farther and faster.

"So, however they are making or creating the baseballs ... they're coming up with a rounder baseball," says sports data scientist Meredith Wills. With a doctorate in astrophysics, her first studies were in publications like the *Astrophysical Journal* and *Solar Physics*. But her most recent research, on the 2019 baseball, appeared June 25th in the online sports publication *The Athletic*.

So how do you make a baseball that's rounder than other baseballs? Wills got her hands on 39 Major League baseballs used in 2019. Compared with last year's ball, "The laces are thinner ... the leather is substantially smoother ... any one of these changes will make the aerodynamics of the ball better, they will decrease the drag. So the way to think of it is that the ball doesn't slow down as quickly when it's traveling through the air, which means that it stays faster longer, which means it's able to travel farther."

Which could account for part of why the players are on pace to hit more than 6,600 homers this year, up from 5,585 last year. Hitters are clearly also changing their swing plane to try to hit more homers, which is probably also a factor. But another indicator of less drag on the ball is home run distance. Wills notes that 82 home runs went at least 450 feet in 2018. This year has already seen 84 of that distance, with almost half a season to play.

The changes in the ball also make it harder for the pitchers to manipulate it. "There are two problems: one is that it becomes harder to grip the ball in a way that allows you to spin it enough to get break, and then the other one is that the height of the seams themselves can affect how much the ball does break, assuming you get it up to the same spin."

Last year, Major League Baseball bought Rawlings, the company that makes the baseballs. So don't be surprised if next year's ball is once again ever-so-slightly less round—to give pitchers a square deal.

About the Author

Steve Mirsky was the winner of a Twist contest in 1962, for which he received three crayons and three pieces of construction paper. It remains his most prestigious award.

Where There's a Wills There's a Way to Explain the Home Run Rise

By Meredith Wills and Steve Mirsky

A strophysicist and sports data scientist Meredith Wills talks about why a subtle change in Major League baseballs may be behind the jump in home runs after 2014.

Steve Mirsky: Welcome to *Scientific American*'s Science Talk, posted on September 30th, 2018. I'm Steve Mirsky. On this episode:

Meredith Wills: A good way to change the drag is to change the spherical symmetry and basically a round revolve is gonna be able to have less drag and therefore travel further so my thought was that the seams are basically the weak points.

Mirsky: That's Meredith Wills (no relation to Maury). She has a doctorate in astrophysics and has authored studies that appeared in the *Astrophysical Journal* and in the journal *Solar Physics*. More recently, she's been studying the game of baseball, as a sports data scientist. On September 19th she published an article in the online publication *The Athletic* about her studies of the baseball itself. In an attempt to figure out why home runs have gone through the roof—from 4,186 home runs in 2014 to 6,105 in 2017. I spoke with Wills by phone.

Home runs are significantly up in Major League Baseball and a lot of actual scientists have been trying to figure out what's going on there so what was it that you were looking for and what did you find out?

Wills: Well, I guess I should point out that this was a question that, in 2017 when it was going on, a lot of people were approaching from a lot of different ways. Some people thought it might be the baseball. Some people thought it might have to do with something called launch angle, just the angle at which the ball is coming off the bat and that there were players who seemed to be altering it and so, therefore, you might get home runs. There were a lot of different approaches and ultimately MLB commissioned a Home Run Committee, which as you say were—the chair is—Dr. Alan Nathan who is a Professor Emeritus of Physics at Illinois. They had engineers. They had mathematicians. They had, you know, it was a very stem-heavy committee and they went through and they did a lot of lab testing and simulations and comparison of data and what they found was that there seemed to be one statistically significant change, which was basically that the baseball itself starting during 2015 but definitely after 2015 had less aerodynamic drag. What they did not find was why they had less aerodynamic drag. Clearly the change was the baseball but the committee itself didn't find a difference in the baseball. I had been doing my research thinking okay, this might have something to do with the baseball and it turns out there's good precedent for that because when changes have been made to the baseball in the past it actually has changed how the ball moves.

The best example of that would be the transition from what's called "the dead-ball era" to "the live-ball era" (you have different eras in baseball) actually corresponded to the change in the source of the wool that was used for the yarn inside the baseball. The inside of a baseball is largely yarn, wrapped around a core and before, during the dead-ball era, all of the yarn was from American sheep but because of World War I, we ran out of wool and we couldn't make baseballs using American wool so we started importing it from Australia. The Australian yarn turned out to behave differently and suddenly you get what's called the live-ball era and people hitting home runs and Babe Ruth and that sort of thing so the actual ball was different because of the wool being different.

Mirsky: American baseballs had Australian wool in them?

Wills: Absolutely.

Mirsky: This is sacrilege.

Wills: Well you know they do ... first of all they do play baseball in Australia so there are Australians out there who might take issue but quite good baseball, in fact. So back to the ball, I thought okay, maybe there's something different about the interior of the ball that was having a similar effect and so what I did was I very, very systematically took apart two samples of baseballs, one that I knew was from 2014 and another set that I knew was from 2016 and 2017. Alan Nathan (back to him) had already established that the change had occurred over 2015 so I could treat 2016 and '17 as a single sample set and this was literally the unlacing the red laces on the baseball and I measured, you know, all sorts of different things: Circumference and mass and you know different factors on the leather, different factors on the yarn inside and there's three different kinds of yarn. I ended with 16 independent variables and I love how science works because this was literally an accidental variable. My 16th variable I didn't even think of until I started doing a different measurement and realized hey, this looks wrong, had to do with the thickness of the laces and thought okay, the thickness looks different between the two populations and, again, it just had to do with the way I was doing a particular measurement and so I went in and I measured the thickness. And there's a way you can do it where you just you know basically wrap the thread around a dowel and you can figure out how many what's called wraps-per-inch or in this case I used centimeters because it's so thin and I found a statistically significant difference in the thickness of the laces between 2014 and 2016 and '17 and it's 9 percent.

And it was a noticeably statistically significant difference. They're thicker now so they're 9 percent thicker now than they were before 2015. And so this turned out to be a really big deal because the only thing that the Home Run Committee had found was that the difference was the ball but they couldn't figure out what was different about the ball. And in fact their particular study *[laughs]* got published about 3 days after I found this result so I spent a couple days sort of you know metaphorically jumping up-and-down saying, "I know the answer, I know the *[laughs]* answer" and ended up, you know, this written up as an article for *The Athletic* and published 2 weeks later saying, "Here's what the difference actually is with the ball, there really is one." Now for most people it seems like thicker laces shouldn't make the ball have less drag because they tend to think that the laces are the same thing as the seams and thicker laces, they would think, gives you higher seams, which should give you more drag, not less.

That's actually a fallacy. It turns out that lace thickness and seam height are 2 different things. I postulated that having thicker laces because they have greater tensile strength they might actually be somehow keeping the ball more spherical than if the laces were thinner and so I did a follow-up study where, instead of using all the baseballs that I had taken apart because obviously I, you know, you can have your cake or you can eat it, *[laughs]* basically. And so I got a new set of baseballs, one of which was, again, pre-2015. The other was post-2015. It was a larger sample set and I hypothesized that if there was an aberration in the spherical symmetry of the ball because a good way to change the drag is to change the spherical symmetry, you know? Basically a rounder ball is gonna be able to have less drag and therefore travel further so my thought was that the seams are basically the weak point. If you're gonna have any deviation from spherical symmetry it's probably gonna be nearer the seams and, on top of that, I thought, okay, thicker laces are more likely to give seams that stay more intact therefore you could get a more spherical ball.

So just taking essentially a set of calipers *[laughs]* I looked at what I called an average diameter, which was essentially points on the ball, and the same points on every one of my baseballs, away from the seams, and then I also looked at diameters, what I called adjacent to the seams so not the seams themselves because they're too high but, like, say, 2 millimeters off, and there's a couple places on the ball where you can measure the diameter and you get a seam adjacent on both sides and what I discovered was that for all, I had 20 balls from before 2015 and what I discovered was that for all 20 of those baseballs they were bulging at the seams. That seam-adjacent diameter was larger than the average diameter, every single baseball from pre-2015 all of which have thinner laces. When you look at the newer baseballs, which have thicker laces, two thirds of them did show some bulging near the seams but not nearly as much and one third of them actually showed essentially un-bulging, as it were, and it was actually narrower near the seams so there wasn't anything systemic in the newer balls and so what it looks like to me is that, yeah, the issue is the seams and the thicker laces are somehow keeping the seams more intact therefore the ball is more spherical and therefore you have less drag, therefore you have more home runs. So it is the laces.

Mirsky: You have a unique background to do this work. You have a doctorate in astrophysics. You do statistical analytics on baseball and you're also an enthusiastic knitter and so you tweeted when you published this in *The Athletic* the other day, you tweeted, "I just realized that reaching this conclusion required a detailed knowledge of physics, baseball and fiber arts. Who would've thought those skill sets would ever come together?"

Wills: I was ... I will admit that thinking about it I was pretty surprised. Part of the detailed knowledge of fiber arts comes from the fact that by knowing how different, different fibers, say, cotton, wool, that's what I mean by different fibers, you know? Polyester counts I guess although we're not discussing that here. I know how they react under different conditions because I do a lot of knitting design. I've done costume design so I've worked, you know, when I say "fiber arts," I mean all sorts of different things. Basically if it involves needles and thread I've ... or yarn, I've done it and cotton reacts in a very particular way when it gets wet, which a lot of people, particularly because we have dryers nowadays don't think about but if you have wet cotton and you distort it somehow and then you let it air dry it actually will retain its shape so we've all had the experience or most of us have had the experience where, let's say, you spill coffee on your shirt during the day and you obviously don't want the coffee stain to stay there so you go into the bathroom and you scrub out your t-shirt in the sink and the divot stays there, you know?

Until you actually take off the shirt and wash it, you've got a divot there for the rest of the day. The reason the divot stays there is because you've distorted the cotton and then you allowed it to air dry, and it takes throwing it back in the dyer to get rid of the divot. The way that the baseballs are made the leather itself—and it makes sense because obviously the leather has to you know conform to the ball, it's gotta get round—gets moistened and then they pulled the red laces, which happened to be made of cotton, through the wet leather so you end up with wet, cotton laces. What they then do and obviously they're pulled super-tight, you know? If you've ever tried to pull the laces out of a baseball or even just tried to pull 'em up with your fingernail they're incredibly tight.

On top of that there is actually a pressure process that goes into once the balls are done to try to flatten the seams so first you have them pulled tight, then you have those seams put under pressure, while they're wet, and then you allow them to dry, all of which is effectively going to stretch out the cotton and for thinner laces, that cotton is gonna stretch more, which means you're gonna have a weaker seam that's more likely to bulge. So that's where the fiber-arts knowledge comes into play. I'm pretty sure ... let's put it this way the Home Run Committee would probably have eventually figured out that the distortion was the seams. The fact that I had the knowledge of what cotton would do, under those circumstances, meant that I was able to get the conclusion much faster.

Mirsky: That's great. I just wanna let people know the names of some of your other publications from earlier in your career: "Statistical Study of Coronal Mass Ejections with and without Distinct Low Coronal Signatures." That's a good example. Let me find another one here.

Wills: There's a few on something called EIT waves, which are basically these large-scale propagating fronts within the corona that I ... that was sort of my specialty but they were named after a particular instrument. I think one of the early terms that was used for them was solar tsunamis, although I believe that's now used for something else so if you've heard the term solar tsunami that would be what were originally referred to as solar tsunamis were those and so I did a lot of the initial work on that. I was the first one for example to come up with an automated detection method for actually tracking these events because they're very dim, the signals-to-noise is terrible and for a long time people would only track them by eye because they thought there was no way that you could deal with the signal-to-noise such that you could actually track the front using your computer and I did it and so that was kind of you know one of my big contributions within solar physics. That also turns out to have carried over well into baseball because now everything is tracking, you know? You're tracking the pitch. You're tracking the ball when it's hit. Now we're actually tracking the players, which I think is really *[laughs]* awesome and that is much more like what I used to do so I'm particularly interested in player tracking partly because it's similar and it's a complex problem, which I like, but also because I'm a total defense geek and so it means that they come together, which was kind of fun.

Mirsky: So player tracking, you're talking about things like route efficiencies?

Wills: Route efficiencies would be one or tracking to see, for instance, a jump when a guy steals a base you know what his ump is like. Player tracking is actually one that is still kind of nascent because, like, route efficiency is a useful one in a way but it's not as useful as people think. Route efficiency is really cool if you have to sprint a really long distance to get the ball. On the other hand if you're playing a normal fly ball, say, having the most efficient route isn't necessarily a good idea because you won't be set up, say, to throw the ball to second base to cut off the runner on first. So there's a lot more subtlety to it.

One of the things that you can pull out of player tracking, which you know again it's nascent, it's still being done, are things like looking at how players set up for, say, that throw or set up for a cut off man or even things like getting multi-player kind of statistics. So how good your first baseman is based on how good the people around him are. Is it that he happens to play the position really well defensively or is it that you have a really, really good infield, meaning you can get away with having a first baseman who can't field the ball or can't catch the ball, I should say?

Mirsky: They're not giving him a lot of bad throws that he has to scoop outta the dirt.

Wills: Right and so you got someone like you know I could throw out names like Todd Helton or Mark Teixeira or whatever people who were incredibly good first basemen who could you know do a half a split or a full split off the bag and feel the bag bounce which meant you could surround them with people who aren't necessarily as good and they can compensate, you know? There's also for instance you can look at efficiency of players running the bases or even just how a player ... it depends on the type of hit but how do they accelerate into first base? There are some guys where their jump is immediate. Ichiro Suzuki was, like, the perfect example of that. I could never figure out how he could be two steps out of the box when he hit the ball but somehow he always seemed to do it or you have guys who are almost still ramping up their speed when they get to first so they don't hit as many singles but once they get going it's easy for them to hit a double, if that makes sense, you know, because they're not sprinters in the same but they absolutely can pick up their speed or even just the route that you take around, you know? If you're running a straight line to first base that's really useful for a single but if you wanna double, you wanna come in at the curve because otherwise you're actually not taking the most efficient route to get to second base if you, essentially, put a right angle from first to second so those are the kinda things that you would track, looking at the players themselves.

Mirsky: Right and you're ... the name of that article that you published in 2008 was "Tracking Large-Scale Propagating Coronal Wave Fronts (EIT Waves) Using Automated Methods" and that has come back to actually be something that your background doing that is helpful now for doing these kinds of tracking of players. It's really amazing.

Wills: Yep and it turns out that the data are less dissimilar than I would've expected, which is kinda fun so it's really cool to be to take one thing and carry it over into another.

Mirsky: And now more with Meredith Wills. We've heard a lot ... if you're a baseball fan, you've heard a lot about exit velocity and launch angle and that players are trying to hit the ball up-in-the-air over the last few years and so most people probably would've assumed that the launch angle had increased but the actual analysis showed that there was no difference in average launch angle between 2014 and 2016 and '17 when there was a big difference in home run rates.

Wills: The important thing to realize is that the home run rates went up globally, you know? It wasn't just that you had a few players who suddenly went from hitting 30 home runs to hitting 55 home runs or something like that, what you had is you had guys who normally hit 10 home runs who were suddenly hitting 15 and everybody was doing it so that's why the numbers went up like that because there was some systematic change throughout the game. There are absolutely players who have changed the way they hit the ball and change their launch angle. A great example would be a couple years ago Daniel Murphy when he was with the Mets during the NLCS and he hit, what, 6 home runs in the 6 games?

Mirsky: Yeah, he hit a home run every day.

Wills: Every game against the Cubs and it was just amazing. I remember that specifically because apparently the goat from the curse was named Murphy and so I was like, okay, well, maybe it's not a goat curse, maybe it's a Murphy curse.

[Laughter]

Wills: You know but anyway the ... at the time everybody thought it was an aberration but by the next year he showed very clearly he had become a power hitter and then explained in interviews that before the postseason, he had actually started working on his swing mechanics to change his launch angle. The thing is though not everybody has done that and even if they've tried, not everybody has been successful. I mean there're some guys who can change their swing mechanics and there're some guys where changing their swing mechanics might just mess with their swing and they probably shouldn't. So in a way looking at something like launch angle you can see it with individual players but to have a global change it would require everybody suddenly deciding to do this and everybody doing it successfully so I think that was ... again, it's a good thing to look into and the Home Run Committee looked into all of this, actually. They had an incredibly ... it's an 80-page report. It's very thorough. It explains a lot and they look at pretty much everything that was postulated during 2017 as far as what, you know?

They looked at essentially, you know, climate change as maybe having an effect with temperatures increasing and therefor the ball might travel further. They looked at launch angle. They looked at ... I think they actually looked at strategy and when you took out all the variables basically what they found was that the ball was traveling further. For a given exit velocity and a given launch angle the ball was traveling further, regardless.

Mirsky: Yeah and there was an observed decrease in drag coefficient that they found as well.

Wills: Yes so when they removed all the rest of the variables that was the only one that stood out as statically significant. There were other changes but not ones ... only things that might show up as trends and nothing that showed up as meaningful. What they were looking for was a genuine change and that was the only statistically significant change was the drag.

Mirsky: And that's what your stitches study tries to account for and may account for.

Wills: Yeah one thing I guess I should point out is with the older balls that are bulging at the seams, baseballs are all made-by-hand and so there does tend to be a fair bit of variation from ball-to-ball so I don't know if we will ... it would take a huge population probably to find a statistically significant difference as far as that bulging effect so, in my case, it's more that the trend is there and that the fact that all of the balls show bulging is telling but for the newer results it's not statistically significant so please, you know, if you're really, really determined to hang your hat on it, that's yours, that's not mine, *[laughs]* you know?

Mirsky: You are proposing a viable hypothesis with this study for the findings of the committee studying home run rates.

Wills: That is an excellent way to put it.

Mirsky: Okay good. I just want people to know the report. It's called "The Report of the Committee Studying Home Run Rates in Major League Baseball" and that's dated May 24th, 2018 and that's available free, for nothing, on the web and your article in *The Athletic* is titled "Studying the baseball to find the 'how' of the home run surge" and *The Athletic* is by subscription. I am fortunate to be a subscriber.

Wills: I should also point out there was a previous. The previous article was published on June 6th and the title is something like "How one tiny change in the baseball may have led to the home run surge and the rise in pitcher blisters," which is a whole different thing. It turns out thicker laces seem to be causing pitcher blisters. We can leave it at that. That's the next study.

Mirsky: This was great. I just find this stuff endlessly fascinating as a science-interested person and a baseball fanatic; I just love all this stuff.

Wills: It is so nice to hear you say that you're a baseball fanatic, having worked with scientists with so much of my life there just aren't enough of us. There should be more.

Mirsky: Going into the last day of the season, we had 5,550 homers in 2018. Not as many as last year's 6,105 but still way up from the 4,186 in 2014.

About the Author

Steve Mirsky was the winner of a Twist contest in 1962, for which he received three crayons and three pieces of construction paper. It remains his most prestigious award.

Blade Runners: Do High-Tech Prostheses Give Runners an Unfair Advantage?

By Larry Greenemeier

Paralympic long jump champ Markus Rehm's bid to compete in the 2016 Rio de Janeiro Olympics fell short in July when he could not prove that his carbon-fiber "blade" prosthesis didn't give him an advantage. His baffling case serves as a reminder that four years after South African sprinter Oscar Pistorius propelled himself into history as the first amputee Olympic athlete to compete using blade prostheses, the technology's impact on performance remains unclear despite ongoing research.

Blade prostheses, like Rehm uses on his right leg and Pistorius used on both, share some characteristics with biological limbs. The blades store energy as they bear the runner's weight and then release it as the runner pushes off the ground, much the way a leg's calf muscles and Achilles' tendons spring and recoil. But an important difference is the foot, which on a blade prosthetic does not pivot or generate its own energy. A biological foot has muscle fibers that help it push off the ground in a way that creates "metabolic efficiency so your muscles don't have to put all of the work back in with every step as you're running," says David Morgenroth, an assistant professor in the University of Washington's Department of Rehabilitation Medicine.

A runner using biological limbs can also adjust the stiffness of leg muscles and the angle at which a foot strikes the ground on the fly to accommodate any changes in a running surface. But the stiffness and shape of a blade cannot be changed once it has been fitted to the runner, as it is custom-optimized for a particular athlete to run under very specific conditions. "That could be a disadvantage when you're trying to get up to speed as a runner, such as when you're coming out of the starting blocks. It's an entirely passive system," Morgenroth says.

The blades do have competitive benefits, however. Once a runner on blades accelerates to top speed, one potential advantage lies in the ability to move the prostheses faster and with less effort—because the blades weigh less than a competitor's lower legs and feet. Researchers who have studied blade prostheses disagree fiercely over the net impact of these pros and cons on overall performance.

The Pistorius Factor

Shortly after track and field's governing body, the International Association of Athletics Federations (IAAF), banned Pistorius in 2008 from competing against so-called "able-bodied" competitors, he underwent a series of tests at Rice University's Locomotion Laboratory in an attempt to be reinstated. The researchers concluded that Pistorius used 17 percent less energy than that of elite sprinters on intact limbs. The tests also revealed that it took the South African 21 percent less time to reposition, or swing, his legs between strides. Big disagreements arose over how to interpret the research.

Southern Methodist University's Peter Weyand and Matt Bundle from the University of Montana saw a clear overall advantage in Pistorius's faster leg swings and more energy-efficient stride, which they said could create up to a seven-second advantage in the 400-meter race. "The more mass you have closer to the axis—in this case, your hips—the easier it is to stop the rotation and then turn it around," Bundle says. "Whereas if you had that same amount of mass located a long way away from the axis—in your lower legs and feet—it becomes much more difficult to stop it and get it going in the opposite direction."

The other researchers—including head of Massachusetts Institute of Technology Media Lab's Biomechatronics research group Hugh Herr, former Media Lab Biomechatronics postdoctoral fellow Alena Grabowski and Rodger Kram, an associate professor in the University of Colorado Boulder's Integrative Physiology Department—determined there was "insufficient evidence" to prove Pistorius's carbon-fiber Flex-Foot Cheetah prostheses gave him an advantage.

Their work helped persuade the Court of Arbitration for Sport to overturn the IAAF ban. The sprinter would go on to compete in the 400-meter and 400-meter relay races at the 2012 Summer Olympics in London.

Leap of Faith in Science

Rehm, whose lower right leg was severely damaged by a boat propeller when he was a teenager, won the German national long jump title in 2014. Officials from Germany's track and field governing body later barred him from competing in the 2014 European Championships in Zurich due to concerns that his blade was creating an unfair advantage. In 2015, as Rehm sought a way to continue competing in mainstream events, the IAAF changed its rules, requiring amputee athletes prove a prosthesis does not give them an edge. In a bid to compete in the 2016 Rio Olympics, Rehm turned to Grabowski, now director of the University of Colorado Boulder's Applied Biomechanics Laboratory, and her colleagues at the German Sport University in Cologne and National Institute of Advanced Industrial Science and Technology in Japan.

Long jumpers such as Rehm rely on a fast run-up sprint followed by an efficient takeoff technique to propel them both vertically and horizontally over a sand pit. During takeoff a jumper lowers his center of mass and pushes off of one leg to quickly get as high in the air as possible without sacrificing forward velocity. In general, the faster the run-up speed the farther a competitor will jump. Grabowski and her colleagues found that Rehm and other world-class long jumpers with a below-the-knee amputation use a fundamentally different technique than competitors who do not need a prosthesis. The blade's passive-elastic nature may limit a jumper's top sprinting speed (a disadvantage) but it enables better takeoff technique (an advantage), Grabowski says. Ultimately the researchers could not say conclusively whether or not Rehm's prosthetic gave him an overall advantage, effectively ending his hopes of competing in Rio. Rehm is now part of an IAAF working group studying prosthesis use in athletic competition, in hopes of competing in the 2017 IAAF World Championships.

Baby Steps

Although Grabowski's long jump study was inconclusive, her research is far from the finish line. In March Grabowski, Kram and research associate Paolo Taboga reported in *The Journal of Experimental Biology* that athletes with a left leg prosthesis are at a disadvantage in track events of 200 meters or more. Having their blade leg on the inside of the counter-clockwise curve made them generally 4 percent slower than those wearing right leg prostheses. The disparity was less pronounced in the outer lanes where the curve radius is not as great. "One of our objectives was to understand how [a] prosthesis affects performance and to—down the line—design better prostheses that could allow someone to negotiate the curves better," Grabowski says.

Grabowski and her colleagues continue to research the effects of blade height and stiffness on performance. After Brazilian sprinter Alan Oliveira beat Pistorius in the 2012 Paralympic Games 200-Meter race, the South African complained that Oliveira's longer blades made him faster. The International Paralympic Committee (IPC), which governs the Paralympic Games, regulates prosthetic length for double-leg amputees based on a number of factors including wingspan (from the tips of one's fingers on one hand to those on the other hand while the arms are held perpendicular to the body) and height. The researchers tested five amputee athletes running at different heights on blade prosthetics made by three companies. "We're actually finding that within a range of four centimeters it's not really having an effect on top speed," Grabowski says. The researchers hope to publish their findings within the next six months.

The question of whether a carbon-fiber prosthetic offers athletes an unfair advantage may never be fully answered, given how much research is still being done to understand what makes a runner—any runner—faster and more efficient, the University of Washington's Morgenroth says. Meticulous lab testing is important but it can never replicate what actually happens on the track in the heat of competition.

About the Author

Larry Greenemeier is the associate editor of technology for Scientific American, *covering a variety of tech-related topics, including biotech, computers, military tech, nanotech, and robots.*

How Paralympic Wheelchairs and Prostheses Are Optimized for Speed and Performance

By Sophie Bushwick

A s audiences across the world tune in to the Tokyo 2020 Paralympic Games, they will see athletes using an impressive array of high-tech prosthetic limbs, wheelchairs and other assistive technology. These devices bear little resemblance to those for everyday use—and vary a great deal from sport to sport.

"We design sporting equipment to get the best possible performance based upon the constraints and needs of that sport," explains Bryce Dyer, a sports technologist at Bournemouth University in England, who develops prostheses for athletes with disabilities.

For example, blade-style prostheses—which are springy to better store and release energy—have become well known in track-and-field events. But people with lower-limb amputations who compete in cycling events have to perform a different type of motion at much higher velocities, so their prosthetic limbs have different requirements. "One of the greatest forces that slow you down when you get above a certain speed is that of aerodynamic drag. And the more drag there is, the more effort you have to apply to try and mitigate for and overcome it," Dyer explains. The legs of nondisabled people are "not particularly aerodynamic; they're not designed for that task. But a cycling prosthesis, we can design it that way." He has created such items with a flat middle section in place of the lower leg. "We can make it very, very thin," Dyer says, "almost like an aircraft wing—razor-blade thickness—to slice through air [and] reduce or remove any turbulence from it." For cycling limbs, this flat section is oriented so the thin edge faces forward, as opposed to blade prostheses for running, in which the broad side does so.

Wheelchairs for different sports also vary widely, although they share some similarities. Many are built from high-tech materials, such as carbon fiber, that make them both strong and lightweight. They often include rubber-coated wheel-turning grips that athletes grab with gloved hands to maximize friction. But beyond that, the designs diverge. In wheelchair fencing, for example, the wheels are locked into place while athletes strike and dodge from set positions. So fencing chairs are equipped with leg straps and sturdy handles that help the athlete stay solidly seated. And many have a lower than usual back to enable more upper-body movement.

The basic shape of a fencing chair still looks a lot like that of an everyday wheelchair. But this is not at all the case with racing chairs, which are built for high speeds. A third wheel in the front of such a device enables a low, elongated shape, which works optimally with the athlete's position: kneeling and leaning forward. Spoked wheels are usually swapped out for smooth disks that generate less air turbulence, reducing the effort required to move at high speeds.

For sports that require more maneuverability, yet another design element is required. "Your tires or your wheels are actually slanted," says retired American wheelchair basketball player Becca Murray, who has participated in three Paralympic Games and won gold at two of them. "And the dynamic of that is that it helps you be faster, and you're able to turn quicker on the dime, whereas your everyday chair—it doesn't let you turn as sharp." Additional wheels on the back of the chair also help with these speedy turns and add stability. But such chairs do sometimes tip over, so designs must be sturdy. This is also why athletes wear straps or belts across their hips and legs. "If you were to fall over, you want to be able to just get right back up," Murray says. "So you want your wheelchair to stay attached to you, almost like you're one with the wheelchair."

In addition to suiting a specific sport, a device must serve each athlete's unique needs. "Most of the equipment is custom-made: it's designed to get the most out of that individual athlete's physical body," says Ian Brittain, an associate professor of disability and Paralympic sport at Coventry University's Research Center for Business in Society in England. For instance, prosthetic legs for track and field may or may not include mechanical knee joints.

"Some runners, depending on the length of their limb, will have a knee joint added" if they have an above-the-knee amputation, Dyer says. "But there are some unique athletes, and a good example of that is the British athlete Richard Whitehead." Whitehead has two above-the-knee amputations and has developed his own running style—one that does not require knee joints at all. "It looks almost like an egg whisk, where he almost brings his legs around in a whisking pattern, left- and right-hand side," Dyer says. "That's very unique to him."

Among athletes who compete in wheelchairs, similar customization is necessary. For instance, increasing the height of the chair's back and the slope of its seat, also called the "dump," can help compensate for abdominal weakness. "I actually have a little dump in my chair because I don't have all my core muscles to help me with that balance," Murray explains. "It just means that my knees are higher than where I'm sitting, so it's on an incline." Players with injuries high on their spine may have less abdominal strength than Murray and require a dump even in their everyday chair. Others with amputations or knee injuries may have more abdominal strength and not need a dump at all.

The technology seen at the Paralympics can increase speed and mobility in sports—but it is unlikely to inspire visibly different designs for nonathletes. One reason is that the wheelchairs used in daily life are already optimized for other qualities, such as taking up as little space as possible. "You want your everyday chair to be the smallest it can be, because in everyday life, you have to get through little places and doorways and things like that," Murray explains. "You like it to fit snug on your hips, and the wheels are straight up and down so that you can be as narrow as possible." Many public spaces are simply not built to accommodate a variety of wheelchair designs.

Price is another consideration. "You have to bear in mind the commercial market for elite athletes is incredibly small, and in many cases, those athletes are sponsored," Dyer says. "So it is important to have some degree of trickle down in the same way that IndyCar or Formula One technology does eventually trickle down to everyday family cars. But sometimes it's quite subtle." For example, some scarcely visible component of a prosthesis—such as the socket that attaches the limb to the wearer's body—may improve.

Plus, Dyer adds, the engineers and designers who work with Paralympic athletes will learn some techniques they can apply to other people with amputations. "It will actually give experience to the prosthetist in how to fit prosthetic limbs to those highly active people—that might wish to jog for recreation, take the dog for a walk, or play tennis or something—in such a way that gives them a greater degree of comfort," he says. "It's not just about how something looks. It's also about the experience that can give prosthetists in creating and designing assistive technology to allow people to perform certain types of activities."

About the Author

Sophie Bushwick is an associate editor covering technology at Scientific American.

Can Science Solve the Mystery of "Deflategate"?

By Sarah Lewin Frasier

Physicist Wanted: On Monday a law firm helping the National Football League investigate the New England Patriots for possible cheating brought out the big scientific guns, calling for Columbia University physicists' help. They needed to determine the extent that the weather conditions at the American Football Conference Championship game on January 18 could have impacted a football's internal pressure and whether it could be to blame for 11 of 12 Patriots footballs being suspiciously underinflated during their trouncing of the Indiana Colts. Apparently, nobody's stepped up yet in an official capacity, but plenty of professional and Monday-morning scientists have taken to the Web to offer their own analyses.

The basic facts, of which I've been blissfully and willfully unaware until now: During the AFC Championship game between the Patriots and the Colts—that determined which team would go on to the Super Bowl, and which the Pats won by a large margin, 45–7—officials found that almost all of the Patriots' footballs were around two pounds per square inch below the regulation pressure range of 12.5 to 13.5 psi, giving them an unfair advantage. (Side Note: Each team's quarterback gets to select his own footballs before the game, and different players have different preferences.)

The balls somehow dropped in pressure between being checked by the referees and halftime—was it foul play? A who's who of the hands footballs pass through before and during a game creates an intriguing list of suspects, but as those avenues of speculation have tired, the curious public has begun to grapple with the science.

First of all, the terminology. People have been fumbling over understanding "pounds" taken off the balls versus "pounds per inch of pressure"—the actual weight difference would have been more like the weight of a dollar bill, according to an ESPN Sport

Science video. Many, including science popularizer Neil deGrasse Tyson, misunderstood the pressure measurement as one of absolute pressure (as if the ball was in a vacuum) rather than gauge pressure, which takes atmospheric pressure into account.

But once that was sorted out, the experiments began. According to chemistry's ideal gas law, reducing the temperature of a gaseous system in a confined space also reduces the pressure of the system—Could nature itself then be the culprit? The basic physics is covered very well in the [ESPN] video by Ainissa Ramirez, materials scientist and co-author of *Newton's Football*, for *Time* magazine—plus, she discusses whether a deflated ball would have offered an advantage to start with.

Ramirez notes that a deflated ball benefits many players: it's easier for a quarterback to grip, a receiver to catch, a runner to carry as well as easier to kick. On the other hand, a deflated ball also doesn't fly as far.

Chad Orzel at *The Conversation*, a physicist at Union College, stuffed footballs in his freezer and found that after a cold night the footballs' pressure had dropped by two pounds per square inch, just like the Patriots' balls. Of course, that was from a temperature drop of 78 degrees Fahrenheit. A blogger named Hondo calculated that the temperature on the playing field would have had to make it down to 31 degrees F to cause the change—much colder than it actually was during the game. Even Bill Nye the Science Guy deduced on video that the temperature alone wouldn't have been enough, although his contribution was mostly dedicated to ranting about climate change while waiting for footballs to chill.

There's always a chance more variables—wear and tear, rain, friction—could have kept the pressure high in the first measurement or lowered it by the second. And even the most basic details could be overturned—What if the other balls weren't as deflated as the first one?—rendering empirical analysis useless. For now the physics has spoken—and we're not much better off. But a national fixation on possible cheating in sports morphing into one on pounds per square inch, gauge pressure and the ideal gas law? That I can get behind.

About the Author

Sarah Lewin Frasier is assistant news editor at Scientific American and editor of the magazine's Advances section.

Building the Ultimate Ultimate Disc

By Laura G. Shields

For almost half my life, I have played the sport of ultimate—previously called ultimate Frisbee—across several states and even internationally, in all types of conditions. On one extreme, the snowy outdoor February tournament in New Hampshire called Live Freeze or Die takes pride in the toughness of its competitors (the name is a takeoff on the state motto, "Live Free or Die"). On the other end, tournaments in the Southwest on scorching turf fields have made me think my feet were melting.

Ultimate only requires one piece of equipment—the disc (not "the Frisbee," which is the trademarked name of the disc made by Wham-O). Players, like me, have noticed that discs fly differently depending on the temperature. In the cold, discs are rigid, painful to catch and break easily. Discs left out in a hot car are floppy and don't fly as well.

For nearly three decades, one company, Discraft, has dominated the disc market. But recently, a small enterprise developed a new disc that's now edging for a spot on the field.

Zahlen Titcomb and his four siblings, founders of the ultimate apparel company Five Ultimate, have thrown and caught discs countless times. Recognizing that players would appreciate a disc that performs better across a wide range of temperatures, they decided to improve the disc on their own.

They also wanted to create a long-lasting disc. Discs may gain dents over use, adding wobbles to their flights.

The problem, however, was the Titcombs didn't know anything about designing a disc. So they started with intuitions of how a disc should feel and perform and progressed with trial and error.

To mass produce a disc, the Titcombs would eventually need a disc mold. Hence, they first experimented with the disc shape. They adhered to the size and weight requirements for official competition approval. They used computer-aided design software and 3D printing to develop different versions. They threw each iteration, advancing toward one with the weight distribution and "rim feel" they preferred.

Next, they focused on the materials. Companies won't reveal their trade secrets, so the five siblings started from scratch. In their initial experiments, they gathered old discs and put them in the freezer and oven to compare how they performed, such as testing how much a disc would bend and return to its original shape. They even looked at other durable products, including dog toys.

Then, they brought the products with properties they liked to engineer friends with access to tools like Fourier-transform infrared spectroscopy to try learning more about the materials. FTIR collects a chemical "fingerprint" of the sample after hitting it with infrared radiation. The radiation passes through or is absorbed by the sample, in a unique way depending on the compounds. This tool helped the team find the general classes of materials used in the products they liked, but it didn't reveal everything.

"It's like trying to unbake chocolate chip cookies," explains Titcomb. "You're never going to figure out what brands of chocolate you started with or how much of this or that flour or whether it was brown sugar or organic brown sugar."

I was curious what these ingredients are, so I reached out to a research professor at Dartmouth University. Rachel Obbard teaches a course on materials in sports equipment. Plastic objects like discs are usually made of a polymer called polyethylene, she says. Additives may include brighteners for coloring, release agents to help remove the item from the mold and ultraviolet protection.

Finally, the designers considered the disc's aesthetics. One source of materials created a disc that appears pockmarked. The disc performed well, but its appearance might turn off the community. Instead, they went for a clean white look.

Two years and 67 prototypes later, Titcomb and his team had a version that worked. They found a combination of fewer, high-quality materials that were crucial for their desired results. Titcomb believes the disc improvements will "allow more people to play in more conditions with a more regular standardized feel and flight path."

I wanted to see how it feels to throw the ARIA disc, so I brought one to my Tuesday night league game in Sunnyvale, California. It was a windless night around 50 degrees, slightly chilly but far from the coldest temperatures I have played in. To warm up, I practiced throwing and catching. It felt like other discs that haven't been thrown before—it flew how I wanted it to.

My throwing partner was Albert Wu, a veteran player of more than 20 years. He actually didn't notice it was a different brand of disc. When I told him afterwards, he was "pleasantly surprised" it was not his normal disc.

And maybe that's the point. The Titcombs want the new disc to feel natural to ultimate players.

Wu, who considers himself a Discraft purist, is not sure he would change to the ARIA disc but noted: "I think if I played with it, I enjoyed it and I couldn't really tell the difference and if it actually played better in cold and hot, I might consider switching over."

I personally look forward to testing its performance in hotter and colder conditions.

In August, the ARIA disc received official approval by the governing national organization, USA Ultimate. It met the size and weight requirements and passed the multilevel player review that tested the flight characteristics.

The timing for this new enterprise couldn't be better. As American youths shy away from the traditional sports such as football and baseball, their participation in non-mainstream sports like ultimate increases. Given ultimate's expansion around the world, the International Olympic Committee is considering adding it to the Summer Olympic Games, as early as 2024.

The disc has transformed significantly from its early days as an inverted pie tin. Perhaps the ARIA disc represents the next stage in the disc's flight throughout history.

About the Author

Laura G. Shields has a Ph.D. in chemistry. She is currently studying science communication at UC Santa Cruz.

The Secret to Human Speed

By Dina Fine Maron

O n a Friday morning this past February champion sprinter Mike
Rodgers got strapped into a safety harness suspended from
the ceiling above a custom-built treadmill. "No one's ever fallen,
but you can be the first," he was told. Rodgers smirked and steeled
himself to run. He was training for the Olympic trials. But that day
he was not completing one of his standard, punishing drills on the
track or in the weight room at his gym. Instead he had showed up
at a small, white building in Dallas with "Locomotor Performance
Laboratory" embossed on the door.

From the outside, the structure looks uninteresting, a converted
printing shop across from a doggy day care and a yoga studio.
But in recent years dozens of sprinters like Rodgers have been
coming by this Southern Methodist University facility to get advice
on their running technique from sports scientist Peter G. Weyand
or to help him with his studies. Weyand has conducted what many
researchers consider to be some of the best science to date on the
biomechanics of sprinting and how these elite athletes achieve their
record-breaking speeds. Ahead of the 2016 Summer Olympics in Rio
de Janeiro, his findings have even been incorporated into training
for top U.S. sprinters.

The heart of the operation is Weyand's treadmill, a roughly
$250,000 contraption outfitted with specialized plates measuring
the force that the runner exerts on the ground during locomotion.
Three cameras positioned around the machine capture high-speed,
3-D images of the user's stride. Rodgers is hoping all these data will
reveal insights that could help him make adjustments that would
shave off crucial fractions of a second in the 100-meter dash.

Clad in the same type of shoes, spandex top and shorts, and
reflective stickers Weyand asks all his subjects to wear, Rodgers
starts to run, loping along at a little more than 6.5 miles an hour to
warm up. Soon, however, he reaches more than 23 miles per hour.

At this pace, the tattoo on his right calf—the cartoon Road Runner with the phrase "Catch me" inscribed below it—is a blur to the naked eye. The equipment feeds measurements into a specialized computer program that graphs his movements.

Weyand has studied more than 120 runners, including 12 other world-class sprinters—observations that have helped fill in a long-standing gap in scientists' understanding of the biomechanics of running at high speed. Before his investigations, the prevailing wisdom about great sprinters was that they are particularly adept at quickly repositioning their limbs for their next step while their feet are in the air. This claim stemmed largely from intuition rather than a theory based on evidence, however. Weyand was the first to test this idea scientifically—and his findings indicate that it is wrong. Instead the key to speed seems to be something else altogether, a factor that Weyand says he can teach sprinters to improve.

On Your Mark

Although running as a sport dates back to at least 776 B.C., when a footrace was the only event in the earliest Olympic Games, the science underpinning it has long lagged far behind. Perhaps the earliest attempt to obtain rigorous data on runners came from British Nobelist Archibald Hill, who in 1927 conducted an experiment in which runners wearing magnets sprinted past large coils of wire that detected the magnets. Knowing the distance between wire coils, he could calculate the velocity and acceleration of the passing runners.

The invention of modern force plates in the 1950s provided the means to study another aspect of running. These devices, which resemble scales, record the amount of weight applied to them and measure it over the course of a stride. With such tools, scientists can examine the changing force exerted by a runner at different speeds during a race or compare the forces from different types of footfalls—those of runners who strike with their heel first versus those who strike toe first, for instance. Italian scientist Giovanni Cavagna gathered force data on runners in the 1970s by having them run over plates set up on a track. But because the plates are so expensive, he had just a few of them—enough to capture data from just a small fraction of a race. To obtain a complete run, Cavagna had to hold multiple races and manually move the plates forward after each one, recording only a few of the runners' steps at a time, which he then cobbled together into a composite picture.

Based on those and other early studies, sprinting science focused primarily on what slows runners down—air resistance, says animal locomotion expert Jim Usherwood of the University of London—as opposed to what speeds them up. On the whole, the work shed little light on what sprinters could do to boost their performance.

Weyand's research has helped shift that focus and generated insights that athletes can act on. But he is not the first to envision such advances. Because speed is the product of stride length times stride frequency, runners presumed that cutting down the amount of time each foot spends on the ground would net greater speed. In 2000 Weyand and his colleagues published a landmark paper showing how it is actually done. They enlisted 33 runners of varying abilities to run on an earlier iteration of their force-plate-equipped treadmill. The results proved surprising. Weyand expected that the feet of faster runners would spend less time on the ground and hence more time in the air than the feet of their slower counterparts. But he did not foresee that regardless of the runners' abilities, they would all take the same amount of time between when a foot lifted off the ground and when that same foot made contact for its next step.

What actually set the great sprinters apart from the rest, Weyand's team discovered, was the force with which the runners hit the ground. In subsequent work, Weyand further determined that at top speeds the best runners landed with a peak force up to five times their body weight, compared with 3.5 times among the average runners. That difference is significant because like a superball that bounces higher the harder it is thrown, a runner who hits the ground with greater force stores up more energy at impact and will travel forward farther and faster as a result, with longer strides. Forceful hits also allow runners to rebound more quickly, reducing the time that feet are touching the ground and thus increasing stride frequency. The best runners have longer, more frequent strides.

Get Set

Recently Weyand's team additionally figured out how the best sprinters are able to generate those higher forces—and in so doing forced a revision of another central tenet of the running world. According to the popular so-called spring-mass model of running mechanics put forward in the late 1980s, the legs of runners move relatively passively, working like pogo sticks to catch the body on hitting the ground and then pushing the body back into the air on rebounding. Graphical representations of the force of their footfall resemble a gentle, symmetrical curve.

But the model is based on observations of runners moving at slower speeds. When Weyand, Southern Methodist physicist Laurence Ryan and biomechanics expert Ken Clark, now at West Chester University, analyzed their video footage and force data, they noticed that the model did not seem to hold for the fastest runners. Instead of contracting and expanding smoothly like pogo stick springs, their legs operated more like pistons, delivering abrupt, intense hits. Force data from their footfall made a tight, tall peak.

Careful study of the lower limbs of these fast runners revealed subtle factors that contribute to the elevated forces they generate: they stiffen the ankle right before they hit the ground, which serves to decelerate the foot and ankle fractions of a second after impact. This deceleration helps to maximize the force exerted on the body by the ground in response to impact and to prevent the loss of that force. Elite sprinters also keep their knees high, maximizing their distance from the ground, which gives them time and space to accelerate their footfall and ultimately land with greater force. The findings, published in 2014, make sense logically, Weyand says: if you hit someone with a limp wrist, it will not have as much force.

Yet if you keep your wrist stiff, then you will pack a better punch, he observes.

Those insights are now informing what the team says to runners and coaches who seek their advice on how to boost sprinting performance. "It's about simple cues. We don't say, decelerate yourself—we say, stay stiff into the ground, and then deceleration will happen because of that," Weyand says. A runner who heeds this advice will feel a harder hit to the ground with each footfall, he adds. The comportment of the rest of the body is also important, including the ankles, knees, hips, torso and head, which should also be kept stiff.

Weyand's findings have not surprised everyone. Biomechanist Ralph Mann, a former Olympic hurdler who now works with runners and coaches at USA Track & Field, had already been giving that type of feedback to runners, says USA Track & Field coach Darryl Woodson, who coaches eight sprinters, including Rodgers. Woodson says having concrete data supporting Mann's advice, however, made coaches "feel more confident in what they told runners."

Go!

Elite athletes who have taken Weyand's tutelage to heart report improvement. Olympic hurdler David Oliver wanted to enhance his performance after he took home the bronze in his event in 2008, so his strengthening coach brought him to Weyand in 2012. Weyand pinpointed Oliver's two weak areas: his feet hit too far from his center of mass, and his knees were too far back—instead of parallel with or ahead of the alternate knee—which limited the force of his hits. Oliver says he focused on those problems in his training and strengthening exercises and saw a consistent improvement after several months. He went on to win the gold medal at a world championship event held in Moscow the following year in the 110-meter hurdles, and he is still fourth on the all-time-greatest list for that event.

But anecdotal reports notwithstanding, no scientific studies on these runners after they have attempted to follow Weyand's advice have been published to date. One analysis currently under way suggests that his recommendations can bring significant benefits, however. Matt Bundle of the University of Montana has been analyzing how the pointers affect volunteer sprinters and has found improvements "on the order of the bump we think people get from performance-enhancing drugs," he says. "It's a pretty dramatic augmentation."

Still, Weyand acknowledges that biomechanics are not the whole story. There are still many areas left to study and things outside of a runner's control, he says. Genetics, for example, are clearly very important. "If you don't have a decent build and muscle properties that will allow you to be forceful, you won't get [great sprinting] done," Weyand explains. And sometimes an athlete can compensate for biomechanical shortcomings: the fastest person ever timed, Usain Bolt of Jamaica, does not execute all his mechanics flawlessly, according to Weyand. That not quite perfect form suggests that other factors must help Bolt's game—especially his height and strength.

Sports scientists observe that Weyand's discoveries apply not just to elite athletes but also to recreational sprinters. Maintaining a stiff ankle, getting knees higher and trying to hit the ground with great force will not make most people Olympians but could help get them to a personal best, they say. Of course, hitting the ground so hard could be problematic for a recreational runner. If a person has poor form, for example, such blows could boost chances of potential injuries, including knee pain, arch pain, shin splints or a condition known as metatarsalgia, in which the ball of the foot becomes inflamed. French researcher JB Morin of the University of Nice Sophia Antipolis recommends running downhill as part of a training regimen designed to keep ankles straight. He also suggests jumping rope to help with quick rebounding. (Weyand's findings apply exclusively to sprinters. Endurance runners cannot hit the ground with as much force, because they instead need to preserve their energy over a longer time.)

For his part, Rodgers is getting good news from Weyand. In general, the best sprinters "attack the ground," according to the sports scientist. Rodgers's force data demonstrated that he already does exactly that. Although he weighs only about 165 pounds, he hit the treadmill with more than 700 pounds of force—and that was when his muscles were tired from a prior workout. There are no guarantees at the Olympics, but if Rodgers qualifies to compete, his assessment bodes well for race day.

About the Author

Dina Fine Maron, formerly an associate editor at Scientific American, *is now a wildlife trade investigative reporter at* National Geographic.

Section 4: Sports Culture

The NFL's Racist "Race Norming" Is an Afterlife of Slavery

By Tracie Canada and Chelsey R. Carter

O n June 2, 2021, the National Football League (NFL) announced it would discontinue the use of race norming–the practice of assuming a lower baseline of cognitive abilities in Black players–in legal settlements for concussion-related injuries. For the past several years, Black former professional football players, led by former Pittsburgh Steelers Kevin Henry and Najeh Davenport, had been speaking out against the practice. Henry, Davenport and colleagues demonstrated that race norming was interfering with their ability to receive compensation and benefits from the settlement. Black retirees, who are overrepresented in the number of former players, staked legitimate claims about their impaired health after risking their minds and bodies for this American sport. Bottom line: the race norming practice limited Black players' access to the compensation they were rightfully owed.

In 2013, the NFL settled for $765 million after more than 4,500 retired players brought concussion-related lawsuits against the league. In theory, approximately 18,000 former players were eligible to receive the settlement, which is meant to cover compensation, medical exams, further research, and legal fees for concussion-related neurological diseases such as dementia, Alzheimer's disease, Parkinson's disease and chronic traumatic encephalopathy (CTE). While this settlement seemed like a victory to some, Black players quickly found out that it would be harder to access these funds because the NFL required that cognitive tests used be adjusted for race. With this in mind, Henry and Davenport quietly filed a lawsuit against the NFL in the fall of 2020.

"Black former players are automatically assumed (through a statistical manipulation called 'race-norming') to have started with worse cognitive functioning than White former players. As a result, if a Black former player and a white former player receive the exact same raw scores on a battery of tests designed to measure their current cognitive functioning, the Black player is presumed to have suffered less impairment, and he is therefore less likely to qualify for compensation," their lawsuit contended.

The June announcement was, rightly, met with shock that the practice had even been in use. But for those of us who are attuned to the actions and strategies of the most profitable and popular professional sport league in the United States, the news wasn't much of a surprise. It is just the latest example on the laundry list of the NFL's anti-Black, racist and discriminatory practices over the past decades. For the NFL, race norming depends on the belief that race is a binary, biological concept, and therefore that differences in Black bodies and minds are not only existent, but quantifiable. But they're wrong on all accounts: race norming is an inherently anti-Black form of scientific racism that is evidence of slavery's afterlife.

As Black feminist anthropologists—one who specializes in sport (Canada) and the other in medicine and public health (Carter)—interested in the social and lived experience of Blackness in the United States, we question how one's interactions with the social world are influenced by one's racialized experiences. The ways that Black football players navigate their time as current and former NFL athletes point to the continued social inequities that plague the league beyond claims of anti-Black racism. This is the same league whose cheerleaders accused it of gender discrimination. A league where only one player on an active roster has felt comfortable disclosing their sexuality as a gay man. A league where only three of 32 head coaches are Black and where some teams maintain racist caricatures as mascots. And a league where Black athletes account for more than 70 percent of the labor force on the gridiron.

When we reconsider the racial demographics of this situation alongside the plantation metaphors that riddle play in the NFL, then the injuries that athletes sustain, especially concussions and their side effects, can be classified, in the words of Saidiya Hartman, as the afterlife of slavery. And these injuries, vis-à-vis concussions and subsequent neurological disorders, are just one of the ways that anti-Blackness will continue to impact athletes long after they retire and are no longer affiliated with their professional teams. Often, these athletes' lives are fundamentally changed by their experience with the sport.

In his investigation of the spectacle and business of hockey, scholar Nathan Kalman-Lamb writes of the structural importance of injury, pain and violence to a team spectator sport. And as despicable a notion as this is, it's true. These are woven into the fabric of football. Largely for this reason, average NFL careers across all playing positions are only 2.66 years long. Thus, the tag "Not For Long," from sociologist Robert Turner's ethnography of NFL athletes, rings true as ever. Given the capitalist impulse of the league, these athletes are cared for just enough to protect the investment that has been made in their labor. NFL teams spent over $500 million on injuries in 2019, but the question becomes, whose bodies, injuries and health matter most to the league?

By requiring race norming to determine neurocognitive impairments in former players, the NFL acted as a racialized organization, as defined by sociologist Victor Ray, legitimizing the unequal distribution of resources to the majority of their players. Not only did this practice extend the NFL's participation in anti-Black practices, it also allowed the league to live up to its capitalist ideals. By 2015, the agreement in the settlement had been updated to nearly $1 billion available for settlement claims funded by the NFL. Even with the NFL's overwhelming financial prominence, race norming was one way the league could more closely moderate who was eligible (read: worthy) for a settlement. Yet, despite its contemporary uses, race norming can be traced back to plantation slavery, eugenics efforts globally and a long history of racial science used to justify the belief in inferior racial groups. These misguided scientific endeavors are rooted in an idea that Black people's bodies are inherently different from white people's bodies.

Scholars Lucia Trimbur, Lundy Braun and Dorothy Roberts have outlined that race norming (also called race correction and ethnic adjustment) and more broadly race-based medicine are not new phenomena. Such statistical practice has been used in medical specialties like pulmonology, neuropsychology, obstetrics, urology and nephrology. Braun's work reveals Thomas Jefferson's "discovery" of differences in pulmonary function between Black enslaved people and white people—rooted in his beliefs that Black enslaved people had lower lung capacity than whites. This "fact" spread and then directly impacted the development of race correction in spirometers—an apparatus still used to measure respiratory disease today.

In nephrology, eGFR, another race-normed test, is the gold standard for measuring kidney function. This test measures levels of creatinine and adjusts for gender, age and race. In 1999, a study developed a statistical prediction equation for eGFR based on race because scientists "determined" that Black people's muscle mass "on average" was higher than white people's—which they argued leads to higher kidney function. This deduction is not only flawed because race is not biological (nor is it genetically linked), but also because the muscle mass of living humans simply cannot be measured feasibly in clinics, according to nephrologist Nwamaka D. Eneanya.

Despite calls from the nation's leading experts to end its use, the test continues to persist. Race norming practices in lung and kidney function mirror the NFL's use of cognitive impairments. The impacts of these anti-Black practices within medicine are not just dire because of potential financial compensation but because there are real consequences on Black people's health and well-being in this country.

Outside of these examples and off the gridiron, these findings about race norming are reminiscent of studies that show bias in pain treatment based on assumptions of biological differences between white and Black patients, unequal COVID-19 treatment and outcomes for Black patients, the ongoing Black maternal health crisis as Black women face higher rates of pregnancy-related deaths, the misdiagnosis of diseases like amyotrophic lateral sclerosis (ALS) in Black patients, and countless other ways that racialized and gendered biases influence the care of historically marginalized groups.

Recently, scientists announced an effort to study the connections between the NFL and ALS, the illness commonly referred to as Lou Gehrig's Disease, after the famous Yankee baseball Hall-of-Famer. As of the writing of this piece, 13 former NFL players have come forward with an ALS diagnosis. In a league where 70 percent of players are Black and nearly 73 percent nonwhite, only two Black men with ALS have come forward, while the other 11 persons with ALS are white. These lopsided ratios suggest the ways that the environment, bias, structural inequities and racial capitalism in slavery's multiple afterlives impact medical diagnosis and care—not simply who gets a settlement from the NFL.

Those who submitted claims for this concussion-related settlement are navigating the NFL's anti-Black afterlife. Concussions are a major component of this, given they are underreported during play and so little is known about their long-term effects in living former players. Through this system, as Hortense Spillers suggests, the bodies of these Black players are reduced from their full humanity to merely flesh. We must continue to examine anti-Blackness in its full extent in order to keep Black bodies from harm, injury and, most importantly, a premature death, as we continue to live in slavery's afterlife.

This is an opinion and analysis article. The views expressed by the author or authors are not necessarily those of Scientific American.

About the Authors

Tracie Canada, Ph.D., is an assistant professor of anthropology and concurrent faculty in Africana Studies at the University of Notre Dame. Her research uses sport to theorize race, kinship and care, gender, and the performing body.

Chelsey R. Carter, M.P.H., Ph.D., is a Presidential Postdoctoral Fellow at Princeton University. Her research investigates how race and racism impact neuromuscular diseases and genetics.

Why Americans Love Baseball and Brits Love Soccer...er... Football

By David Papineau

T he start of the year is a good time for American sports fans. The familiar contests follow one another in quick succession. The Super Bowl and March Madness, Opening Day and the Masters, the NBA and NHL playoffs. These old sporting friends come round each year with a pleasing regularity.

The Nobel-prize-winning novelist J.M. Coetzee is a big sports enthusiast. At one point in a published series of letters between him and Paul Auster (*Here and Now* 2013) he raises an interesting question. Why do no new sports get invented any more? Nearly every well-known sport had its rules codified in the second half of the nineteenth century. Since then, scarcely any new sports have emerged. So what blocks their creation?

In keeping with his day job as a professor of literature, Coetzee wonders whether the number of viable sporting forms is limited. Perhaps some deep structure of games allows only a restricted range of constructions from a universal sporting grammar.

I'd say that Coetzee's suggestion is belied by the rich variety of sports that can be found in different parts of the world. There seems no limit to the arrangements that humans can devise to test their physical prowess. Rather, the real problem facing any newly invented sport is its lack of tradition.

History is an essential component of sports. All established sports can tell tales of past heroes and famous victories. This adds to the significance of athletic achievement. It is one thing to be good at hitting a leather ball with a big stick. It is another to follow in the footsteps of Babe Ruth and Ted Williams, of Jackie Robinson and Joe DiMaggio.

Intellectual commentators often bemoan cultural imperialism. Hollywood films and English-speaking TV are swamping the world,

121

they complain, eliminating local traditions and turning everything into a homogenized cultural soup.

I wonder how many of these intellectual pessimists are sports fans. They might be right about some aspects of mass-market media—though if you ask me they would do well to get out more—but they are certainly wrong about sports. Each region of the world has its own sporting traditions, and there is little evidence that they are under any threat.

If you turn on the television on a winter's Saturday morning in Melbourne, Australia, you are likely to see a group of large men engaged in earnest conversation. They are dissecting the afternoon's upcoming "footy" matches, analyzing possible tactics, rating the players, measuring them against past titans like Ted Whitten, Bob Skilton, and Ron Barassi.

You would be hard put, given the gravity of their demeanor, to tell that the game of which they speak is little played outside their city. In Melbourne, "football" means Australian Rules Football, a very specific variety of the genus, played on a huge oval field with eighteen players a side. The main clubs take their names from Melbourne suburbs, and the annual Grand Final attracts a crowd of 100,000.

However, in Sydney, the nearest big city, and Brisbane, the next one north, "football" refers to a quite different game. Here it is Rugby League, a thirteen-a-side contest that is itself largely peculiar to the east coast of Australia and the north of England. It is not dissimilar to the more widespread fifteen-a-side Rugby Union code, but is distinguished by its history of professional players and working-class roots.

In Sydney, Aussie Rules is viewed as a quaint southern oddity, and it is the League heroes that obsess the media. In 2014 the League Grand Final between South Sydney "Rabbitohs" and the Canterbury "Bulldogs" filled the huge ANZ Stadium and attracted a TV audience of 4.6 million. The Rabbitohs' victory was a triumph for their owner, film star Russell Crowe, whose backing had taken the struggling inner-city team to their first Final victory in 43 years.

And so it goes. The term "football" is itself a testament to the diversity of sporting traditions. Melbourne and Sydney are not the only places that attach their own meaning to the word. In much of the world, of course, it stands for the round-ball game technically designated as Association Football. But in Ireland it is generally understood as meaning Gaelic Football, in New Zealand it is traditionally used for Rugby Union, while in North America it refers to the gridiron version of the game.

Each region of the world has its own sporting traditions, and they are not easily dislodged. Evangelical sports entrepreneurs periodically try to export their home games to new markets, but their initiatives are typically ineffective. The American NFL plays some of its games in London each year, but few locals pay much attention. Similarly, Major League Baseball held the first game of the season in Australia for a while, but now seem to have given this up as a bad job.

In truth, sporting traditions reach too deep to be uprooted by marketing exercises. They are passed on from generation to generation, and command a loyalty that is central to many people's identity. From an early age, youngsters acquire sporting heroes, team affiliations, and an ingrained sense of how their games should be played. These are not things that you can learn from an advertising campaign.

So it is no accident that the American sporting calendar remains constant from year to year, featuring the same games in the same formats, with only minimal changes. The answer to Coetzee's question is that modern sports command allegiance because of their histories. Back at the beginning of the industrial age, space on the sporting map was up for grabs, and it was still possible to devise new sporting disciplines. But that era is long gone. Each region of the world now has its own sporting traditions, and will not relinquish them lightly. For sports fans, the historical resonance of their local games adds meaning to their lives.

About the Author

David Papineau is a professor of philosophy at the City University of New York Graduate Center and at King's College London. His books include Introducing Consciousness *(Icon Books, 2001),* Philosophical Devices: Proofs, Probabilities, Possibilities, and Sets *(Oxford University Press, 2012), and* Knowing the Score *(Basic Books, 2017), which takes a philosophical perspective on sporting issues.*

What Does Success Mean for Long-Suffering Sports Fans? An Identity Crisis, Say Researchers

By Eric Simons

In August 1987, in the midst of one of the darkest periods in English soccer history, a countercultural movement sprung into existence in the stadium of the Manchester City Football Club when a man named Frank Newton brought a five-foot inflatable banana to a game for a laugh. Laughs being rare in the stands at that time, other fans embraced the idea of inflatable bananas and a trend bloomed. Vendors started selling them. Newton himself soon switched to a six-foot inflatable crocodile, according to a definitive account at the Manchester City fan newsletter MCIVTA. Other fans hoisted inflatable sharks, airplanes, and wading pools.

This craze was exactly the sort of thing one might expect of Manchester City fans, lovable losers who had invented their own methods of coping with a team notorious for weird failure. The team had bounced around between leagues and hadn't won an English championship since 1968, but the fans' sense of dark humor made them resilient and loyal.

In 2012, four years after a private equity firm owned by a billionaire member of the royal family of Abu Dhabi bought MCFC, the team won a Premier League title for the first time since 1968. The team won it again in 2014. And while there was much joy at the end of such a long title-drought, there was also some head shaking. Fans had gone from being famously persistent losers, supporters of everyone's second-favorite team, to being front-runners, supporters of one of the world's most valuable and successful sports teams. "Success has come but I think many older fans feel strangely conflicted by now being one of the teams-to-beat," ESPN FC Managing Editor Steve Busfield told me a few years ago, when I

125

was conducting research for my book about sports fan psychology. "City fans used to be joyful in their misery."

Which brings me to the resurgent New York Mets, and their fans. When Frank Newton brought his inflatable banana to Manchester, the Mets were the defending World Series champions. They haven't won it since, but now, the franchise commonly tagged #LOLMets, finds itself one of the two most successful teams in baseball. They're behind in the World Series this year as it moves to New York for Game 3 on Friday; but win or lose, they have a talented roster and great young pitchers. They're already the National League champions, and there's no real reason to think this year's success will be a one-off event. Psychologically, does it mean anything for fans accustomed to defining themselves as "not the Yankees" to suddenly start winning? Say the Mets winning streak continues for another few years and winning's not a miracle anymore: does the experience of being a fan change?

Mets fans resemble pre-2012 Manchester City fans. (Disinterested armchair theorist disclosure: I'm neither.) They're eminently lovable to those of us who don't love the Mets. It's an affiliation that allows one to be a sports fan, but not really one of *those* sports fans. For example, think about how different it would be on the *Daily Show* if Jon Stewart had always talked about his Yankees fandom. To call yourself a Mets fan is an obvious demonstration of personal loyalty: if you're wearing a Mets hat, you're obviously not a fickle front-runner. You can—or could—trust a Mets fan.

People are motivated to be sports fans for a variety of reasons, according to Murray State psychologist (and Kansas City Royals fan) Daniel Wann. One reason is that winning produces an increase in the fans' self-esteem. There are a lot of very interesting ways to explain *why* this happens; for now, let's just assume it does. So Mets fans, whether they've suffered every insult since 1987 or joined the bandwagon this year, enjoyed a nice sense of well being following the team's defeat of the Cubs. If the team comes back to win the World Series, fans will enjoy another round.

There are also theories of pride, such as the one advanced by psychologists Lisa Williams and David DeSteno, that suggest that pride is just externally validated self-esteem, which is to say, when you know you've done a good job and you know that others know you've done a good job, you become more prideful. Williams and DeSteno suggest that this explains the evolutionary origins of pride: it's there to help you persist in dull tasks with delayed payoffs. Winning on national television means that Mets fans, again, regardless of the duration of their fandom, should also feel pride.

For bandwagon fans, who've joined up this year, that's essentially the extent of the payoff. They'll experience, in the moment, self-esteem, pride, happiness, entertainment, fun–and no emotional or psychological complications. This is a great argument for being a bandwagon fan, and also one of the reasons we're so frustrated by them–our keen sensitivity to freeriders makes us skeptical of people who are receiving communal benefits without having put in the suffering.

Why would anyone stick with a losing team, then? The case of the Manchester City fans and their bananas suggests one way of thinking about it. Sports fandom is one of the more accessible, more obvious, more fixed sources of identity out there in the world. Win or lose, the existence of the relationship props you up. A sports team and its fanbase are an anchor point in an inconstant universe, fulfilling a need for belonging that, some researchers argue, is as fundamental a motivator to us as hunger.

Winning can, beyond the fans' control or even desire, reshape the identity of the group the devotees belong to. Older Manchester City fans delighted, of course, in the championships, but also felt some mixed-up sense of loss about the new version of the club– and its fans–that wasn't quite like the old one they'd fixed their personal star to. Red Sox fans after the team won the World Series in 2004 and 2007 suddenly became, to everyone else, no different than the overconfident supporters of the archrival Yankees. Golden State Warriors fans, long among the most loyal and most likable in the NBA, have reacted with endearing astonishment to find that, after the team won its first title since 1975 earlier this year, lots of people suddenly intensely dislike them. This identity crisis has a parallel, I believe, in the emotions of empty-nester parents dropping a child off at college. *We've come such a long way and succeeded! But ... we're not the parents of a dependent anymore.*

Identities change, of course. But as one sports fan sociologist pointed out to me, there's a reason that the perpetually losing football team leaving Cleveland for Baltimore in 1996 was treated by many fans as the equivalent of a death in the family. The identities we vest in sports teams matter, and it's hard on fans when that source of identity is taken from them.

People dismiss sports fans and the emotions they inspire, but an understanding of how people behave, and the various ways with which they connect—and multidisciplinary lines of evidence from psychology, neuroscience, endocrinology, and sociology—suggest there's no affectation and no theft of undeserved glory here. The team wins; the euphoria is totally real. This is your brain reveling in what it senses and processes as its own monumental accomplishment.

But with persistent success the euphoria fades, and fans confront the next question: who am I now?

You wouldn't trade the success, just as you wouldn't want your college kid returning to diapers and spitting on you. But sometimes even the successful parent would just like to be—for a few minutes—the person who woke up three times a night to soothe a crying baby, who didn't know it would all turn out okay but persisted anyway in the hope that someday it might. Sometimes the successful sports fan, the winner, pulls the inflatable banana out of the closet and thinks about it, and the person who carried it, and what it meant, and doesn't mean anymore.

About the Author

Eric Simons is the author of The Secret Lives of Sports Fans: The Science of Sports Obsession *(Overlook Press, 2013). He is also the editorial director at* Bay Nature *magazine in Berkeley, California.*

The Surprising Problem of Too Much Talent

By Cindi May

Whether you're the owner of the Dallas Cowboys or captain of the playground dodge ball team, the goal in picking players is the same: Get the top talent. Hearts have been broken, allegiances tested, and budgets busted as teams contend for the best athletes. The motivation for recruiting peak performers is obvious—exceptional players are the key to team success—and this belief is shared not only by coaches and sports fans, but also by corporations, investors, and even whole industries. Everyone wants a team of stars.

While there is no denying that exceptional players like Emmitt Smith can put points on the board and enhance team success, new research by Roderick Swaab and colleagues suggests there is a limit to the benefit top talents bring to a team. Swaab and colleagues compared the amount of individual talent on teams with the teams' success, and they find striking examples of more talent hurting the team.

The researchers looked at three sports: basketball, soccer, and baseball. In each sport, they calculated both the percentage of top talent on each team and the teams' success over several years. For example, they identified top NBA talent using each player's Estimated Wins Added (EWA), a statistic commonly employed to capture a player's overall contribution to his team, along with selection for the All-Star tournament. Once the researchers determined who the elite players were, they calculated top-talent percentage at the team level by dividing the number of star players on the team by the total number of players on that team. Finally, team performance was measured by the team's win-loss record over 10 years.

For both basketball and soccer, they found that top talent did in fact predict team success, but only up to a point. Furthermore, there was not simply a point of diminishing returns with respect to top talent, there was in fact a cost. Basketball and soccer teams with the greatest proportion of elite athletes performed worse than those with more moderate proportions of top level players.

Why is too much talent a bad thing? Think teamwork. In many endeavors, success requires collaborative, cooperative work towards a goal that is beyond the capability of any one individual. Even Emmitt Smith needed effective blocking from the Cowboy offensive line to gain yardage. When a team roster is flooded with individual talent, pursuit of personal star status may prevent the attainment of team goals. The basketball player chasing a point record, for example, may cost the team by taking risky shots instead of passing to a teammate who is open and ready to score.

Two related findings by Swaab and colleagues indicate that there is in fact tradeoff between top talent and teamwork. First, Swaab and colleagues found that the percentage of top talent on a team affects intrateam coordination. For the basketball study, teams with the highest levels of top performers had fewer assists and defensive rebounds, and lower field-goal percentages. These failures in strategic, collaborative play undermined the team's effectiveness. The second revealing finding is that extreme levels of top talent did not have the same negative effect in baseball, which experts have argued involves much less interdependent play. In the baseball study, increasing numbers of stars on a team never hindered overall performance. Together these findings suggest that high levels of top talent will be harmful in arenas that require coordinated, strategic efforts, as the quest for the spotlight may trump the teamwork needed to get the job done.

The lessons here extend beyond the ball field to any group or endeavor that must balance competitive and collaborative efforts, including corporate teams, financial research groups, and brainstorming exercises. Indeed, the impact of too much talent is even evident in other animals: When hen colonies have too many dominant, high-producing chickens, conflict and hen mortality rise while egg production drops. So before breaking the bank to recruit superstars, team owners and industry experts might want to consider whether the goal they are trying to achieve relies on individual talent alone, or a cooperative synergy from the team. If the latter, it would be wise to reign in the talent and focus on teamwork.

About the Author

Cindi May is a professor of psychology at the College of Charleston. She explores mechanisms for optimizing cognitive function in college students, older adults, and individuals with intellectual disabilities. She is also the project director for a TPSID grant from the Department of Education, which promotes the inclusion of students with intellectual disabilities in postsecondary education.

To Win a Sports Bet, Don't Think Too Much

By Cindi May

It's summertime. For Americans, that means baseball season and all the simple pleasures that the game affords—from peanuts and Cracker Jack to the seventh inning stretch and renditions of "Take Me Out to the Ballgame." For many, though, the game is not the same without the opportunity to place a little (or even a big) wager on the outcome. Whether legal or not, betting is ubiquitous in baseball, and in all other sports for that matter. And of course betting is not even limited to sporting events: it has evolved into an international, multi-billion dollar industry. People now wager on the outcome of events like American Idol and the Miss American Pageant just as readily as they do the World Series or March Madness.

Given the prevalence of betting and the money at stake, it is worth considering how we pick sides. What is the best method for predicting a winner? One might expect that, for the average person, an accurate forecast depends on the careful analysis of specific, detailed information. For example, focusing on the nitty-gritty knowledge about competing teams (e.g., batting averages, recent player injuries, coaching staff) should allow one to predict the winner of a game more effectively than relying on global impressions (e.g., overall performance of the teams in recent years). But it doesn't.

In fact, recent research by Song-Oh Yoon and colleagues at the Korea University Business School suggests that when you zero in on the details of a team or event (e.g., RBIs, unforced errors, home runs), you may weigh one of those details too heavily. For example, you might consider the number of games won by a team in a recent streak, and lose sight of the total games won this season. As a result, your judgment of the likely winner of the game is skewed, and you are less accurate in predicting the outcome of the game

132

than someone who takes a big picture approach. In other words, it is easy to lose sight of the forest for the trees.

Yoon and his research team explored the optimal process of prediction in a series of studies examining bets made on soccer matches and baseball games. In their first study, they reviewed more than one billion (yes, billion) bets placed in 2008-2010 through Korea's largest sports-betting company, "Sports ToTo." They characterized the bets in one of two ways: (a) bets that involved a general prediction (i.e., win or lose), and (b) bets that involved a specific prediction (i.e., a precise score). Critically, they wanted to know which type of bet was more likely to result in an accurate prediction of the overall winner. Despite the fact that the specific bets were arguably more difficult and involved greater effort than general bets, they led to diminished success in predicting the global outcome of the game (i.e., which team won). This disadvantage was especially pronounced for games in which the favored team won.

These findings suggest that adopting a holistic approach when predicting outcomes, even for multi-faceted events like sporting competitions, may be more effective than dwelling in the details. However, because these findings reflect performance in a natural setting, they are open to alternative interpretations. For example, different kinds of people (e.g., risk-averse versus risk-seeking) may be more prone to placing different kinds of bets (e.g., general versus specific). In addition, different opportunities for reward may influence betting behavior, thus encouraging those making specific bets to take risks on unlikely outcomes. To control for these factors, Yoon's team examined betting behavior in a controlled laboratory paradigm.

In three different experiments, participants were asked to make predictions about upcoming sporting events. In each study, half of the participants were randomly selected to make general win/lose predictions, while the other half were asked to make specific score predictions. The dependent measure was the same for both groups: Could they predict the winners?

The pattern of performance across the three studies was remarkably consistent: Participants who made general win/lose predictions were reliably better at projecting the winners of the sporting events than those who made specific score predictions. This advantage was evident regardless of whether reward opportunities were relative (i.e., only the participant with the highest overall performance received cash) or individual (participants received cash for every correct prediction).

Notably, experts did outperform novices. Nonetheless, even experts were reliably better in predicting winners when making general bets than when making specific bets. It seems that even in cases where greater knowledge may offer an advantage, the act of focusing on that knowledge can disrupt decision-making. Thus, while a lifelong baseball fan is more likely to pick the winning team than someone who has never watched a game, for either person a quick prediction about the winner is likely to be more accurate than one that follows deep reflection.

Yoon's team confirmed this notion by assessing the kinds of information participants were using to make their predictions. As you might expect, those assigned to the general win/lose group reported relying on global assessments (e.g., overall impression of the teams, performance of the teams in years past) to a greater extent than those assigned to the specific score group. In addition, reliance on global information significantly predicted success for all participants. Even for those in the specific score group, use of detailed knowledge (e.g., strength of the defense, coaching talent) was not associated with better performance, while use of global information was.

These data align with lessons learned from research on basic personal decisions. Whether choosing a jelly bean flavor, rating the attractiveness of a face, or selecting a poster to hang in a room, people are more satisfied with their selection and less likely to change their minds when they make their decisions quickly, without systematically analyzing their options or mulling over the reasons for their choice. The advice is thus the same whether considering complex scenarios or simple situations: Don't overthink it.

Today, more than ever before, we have access to extensive data that we can consider when making complicated decisions like selecting a mutual fund or betting on a baseball series. While reviewing that information may prove useful in developing an accurate overall view of the options, the results from Yoon and colleagues suggest that focusing on the details during the decision process will prove detrimental. It is best to trust your instincts and make up your mind already.

About the Author

Cindi May is a professor of psychology at the College of Charleston. She explores mechanisms for optimizing cognitive function in college students, older adults, and individuals with intellectual disabilities. She is also the project director for a TPSID grant from the Department of Education, which promotes the inclusion of students with intellectual disabilities in postsecondary education.

So, You Want Your Toddler to Grow Up to Win a Gold Medal

By David Z. Hambrick

Early specialization—encouraging kids to focus on mastering a single activity from a very early age—is a striking trend in today's culture. Replacing Tiger Woods, the current poster child for this approach to training is the skier Mikaela Shiffrin, winner of the Olympic gold medal in the giant slalom earlier this month. Reading books such as Daniel Coyle's *The Talent Code*, which argues that the idea of natural-born talent is a myth, Shiffrin's parents developed a plan to gradually improve her skill. Shiffrin was on skis at age 2, and her life has revolved around skiing ever since.

The logic of early specialization is straightforward: Training is necessary to develop skill, but there is a limit to how much a person can train, not just because there are only 24 hours in a day, but because training is physically and psychologically exhausting. A person can train intensively for only a few hours a day without injuring themselves or getting burned out. Thus, the child who starts training early will have a virtually insurmountable training advantage over the child who starts later. Training is, of course, necessary to develop skill. However, the findings of a study recently published in the *Journal of Sports Sciences* show that *later* specialization may actually lead to better performance in the long-term.

Professor Arne Güllich, director of the Institute of Applied Sport Science at the University of Kaiserslautern in Germany, compared the training histories of 83 athletes who medaled in the Olympics, or a World Championship event, to those of 83 athletes who competed at that level but did not medal. (The groups were matched on age, gender, and sport to control for any influence of these factors on the results. For every medalist in a given event, the sample included a non-medalist in that event of the same gender and roughly the same age.) The results showed that both the medalists and non-medalists started practicing in their main sport before the age of 12. However, the medalists started training in their main sport an average of 18 months later than the non-medalists. (The medalists started at age 11.8, on average, compared to age 10.3 for the non-medalists.) The medalists also accumulated significantly less training in their sport during adolescence and significantly more training in *other* sports. This pattern of results held across a wide range of sports, from skiing to basketball to archery.

Along with reducing the risk of burnout and injury, allowing children to sample a range of activities before specializing allows a process known as *gene-environment correlation* to operate to its full extent. This is the idea that our genetically-influenced traits have an influence on the environments that we seek out and create for ourselves. As recently argued by the behavioral geneticist Elliot Tucker-Drob, gene-environment correlation is fundamental to understanding how expertise develops in children. For example, given the opportunity to try several sports, a child may discover that she has a high level of physical endurance and gravitate towards soccer because it places a premium on this attribute. She may also prefer soccer over other sports because she is extroverted and enjoys having teammates. In turn, after some initial success in the sport, the child's coach may encourage her to continue playing soccer, setting in motion a "virtuous cycle" of effort followed by improvement, followed by further effort and improvement. However, this natural selection process will never unfold if the child isn't given ample opportunity to try several sports before specializing.

A likely reason why the early specialization approach has become so popular is that stories like those of Tiger Woods and Mikaela Shiffrin are so compelling. These anecdotes reinforce the belief that practically anyone can become a champion with the "right" environment. At the same time, it is possible that Woods and Shiffrin just happened to specialize in the "right" sport—one that matched their penchants and preferences. In other words, where the selection of a sport was concerned, they may have gotten lucky. Had they chosen another sport, they may not have been nearly so successful.

Anecdotes are inadequate to make sound decisions about how best to train kids in sports and other activities. What is needed—and what is emerging through research by Arne Güllich and other sports scientists—is a body of empirical evidence that parents, teachers, and coaches can use as a basis for making decisions that will not only help youth reach the highest level of performance they can, but also maximize their enjoyment and minimize the risk of a host of negative outcomes.

About the Author

David Z. Hambrick is a professor in the Department of Psychology at Michigan State University. His research focuses on individual differences in cognition and the development of expertise.

Sports Results Affect Voter Behavior

By Karen Hopkin

Local college football wins before elections upped incumbents' vote totals, and college basketball wins influenced presidential ratings. Karen Hopkin reports:

W hen it comes to elections, sometimes we vote with our heads and sometimes with our hearts. But scientists at Stanford say we might also be voting with our pompoms. Because they've found that our behavior at the polls is influenced by the results of local sporting events, work published in the *Proceedings of the National Academy of Sciences*.

Humans are emotional creatures. And our strong feelings about one thing can spread to another. So the Stanford scientists wondered whether events that are unrelated to government performance might sway the way people feel about their elected officials. And what could be less relevant to the workings in Washington or your state capital than college football?

The researchers looked at the election results from 20 years' worth of presidential, senatorial and gubernatorial races. And they found that a home-team win before the election gave the incumbent a boost of almost two percentage points. The more beloved the team, the bigger the bounce.

And it's not just football. In a separate survey, the scientists found that NCAA college basketball results affected presidential approval ratings. So next election day, you might think about practicing a little separation of stadium and state.

Taming the Madness of Crowds

By Gary Stix

I t is called "football crowd disorder" in the academic literature. On the street, it's known simply as hooliganism. The melees at international soccer matches are infamous for the intensity of violence. Among the worst was the rioting that killed 39 fans at Belgium's Heysel Stadium during a 1985 match between English and Italian clubs. To keep public order, many countries flood big games with police in full riot gear. But the hard-line display of uniforms, helmets and batons often has the opposite effect, acting as a spark that incites disturbances.

Social scientists who study hooligan chaos think they have found a better way to keep the peace. Last year Clifford Stott of the University of Liverpool in England and his colleagues published in *Psychology, Public Policy, and Law* a paper that relates a giant experiment at the Euro2004 championship finals. There Portuguese security adopted the researchers' recommendation to institute low-profile, nonaggressive tactics—the most visible of which was to leave the riot gear behind for police officers closest to fans. "We had a working hypothesis that predicted what would happen, but we had never had an entire European nation implement a style of policing based on our predictions," Stott says.

The Portuguese deployed on average seven police near every 100 fans during high-risk matches as compared with one officer for every two fans at Euro2000 in the Netherlands and Belgium. One English fan among the 150,000 at Euro2004 was arrested for violent offenses as against nearly 1,000 of the English contingent at Euro2000. (Stott's team tracked the English spectators closely because fans of that nation are so intimately associated with soccer hooliganism.)

The laissez-faire style, the team contends, did not alienate fans in the same way that legions of police in riot gear do. Shows of force, it seems, tend to antagonize crowds, especially if police display favoritism, as in the case of a 2001 match in Rome when the officers stood by while Italian fanatics pelted Manchester United aficionados with full plastic bottles.

Stott and his colleagues are now involved in a European Union–sponsored project to implement these policing methods in almost all member countries. If they are successful, European fans would feel the sting only of their team's loss, rather than that of tear gas.

About the Author

Gary Stix is a senior editor at Scientific American.

Trans Girls Belong on Girls' Sports Teams

By Jack Turban

In February 2020, the families of three cisgender girls filed a federal lawsuit against the Connecticut Association of Schools, the nonprofit Connecticut Interscholastic Athletic Conference and several boards of education in the state. The families were upset that transgender girls were competing against the cisgender girls in high school track leagues. They argued that transgender girls have an unfair advantage in high school sports and should be forced to play on boys' teams.

Conservatives around the country have jumped on the question. Attorney General Merrick Garland was pressed on the issue during his confirmation hearing last month. State legislators around the country are pushing bills that would force trans girls to compete on boys' teams. In describing the Connecticut case in the *Wall Street Journal*, opinion writer Abigail Shrier expressed a representative argument: when transgender girls compete on girls' sports teams, she wrote, "[cisgender] girls can't win."

The opinion piece left out the fact that two days after the Connecticut lawsuit was filed by the cisgender girls' families, one of those girls beat one of the transgender girls named in the lawsuit in a Connecticut state championship. It turns out that when transgender girls play on girls' sports teams, cisgender girls can win. In fact, the vast majority of female athletes are cisgender, as are the vast majority of winners. There is no epidemic of transgender girls dominating female sports. Attempts to force transgender girls to play on the boys' teams are unconscionable attacks on already marginalized transgender children, and they don't address a real problem. They're unscientific, and they would cause serious mental health damage to both cisgender and transgender youth.

Policies permitting transgender athletes to play on teams that match their gender identity are not new. The Olympics have had trans-inclusive policies since 2004, but a single openly transgender athlete has yet to even qualify. California passed a law in 2013 that allows trans youth to compete on the team that matches their gender identity; there have been no issues. U SPORTS, Canada's equivalent to the U.S.'s National Collegiate Athletic Association, has allowed transgender athletes to compete with the team that matches their identity for the past two years.

The notion of transgender girls having an unfair advantage comes from the idea that testosterone causes physical changes such as an increase in muscle mass. But transgender girls are not the only girls with high testosterone levels. An estimated 10 percent of women have polycystic ovarian syndrome, which results in elevated testosterone levels. They are not banned from female sports. Transgender girls on puberty blockers, on the other hand, have negligible testosterone levels. Yet these state bills would force them to play with the boys. Plus, the athletic advantage conferred by testosterone is equivocal. As Katrina Karkazis, a senior visiting fellow and expert on testosterone and bioethics at Yale University explains, "Studies of testosterone levels in athletes do not show any clear, consistent relationship between testosterone and athletic performance. Sometimes testosterone is associated with better performance, but other studies show weak links or no links. And yet others show testosterone is associated with worse performance." The bills' premises lack scientific validity.

Claiming that transgender girls have an unfair advantage in sports also neglects the fact that these kids have the deck stacked against them in nearly every other way imaginable. They suffer from higher rates of bullying, anxiety and depression—all of which make it more difficult for them to train and compete. They also have higher rates of homelessness and poverty because of common experiences of family rejection. This is likely a major driver of why we see so few transgender athletes in collegiate sports and none in the Olympics.

On top of the notion of transgender athletic advantage being dubious, enforcing these bills would be bizarre and cruel. Idaho's H.B. 500, which was signed into law but currently has a preliminary injunction against its enforcement, would essentially let people accuse students of lying about their sex. Those students would then need to "prove" their sex through means including an invasive genital exam or genetic testing. And what happens when a kid comes back with XY chromosomes but a vagina (as occurs with people with complete androgen insensitivity syndrome)? Do they play on the boys' team or the girls' team? This is just one of several conditions that would make such sex policing impossible.

It's worth noting that this isn't the first time people have tried to discredit the success of athletes from marginalized minorities based on half-baked claims of "science." There is a long history of similarly painting Black athletes as "genetically superior" in an attempt to downplay the effects of their hard work and training.

Recently, some have even harkened back to eras of "separate but equal," suggesting that transgender athletes should be forced into their own leagues. In addition to all the reasons why this is unnecessary that I've already explained, it is also unjust. As we've learned from women's sports leagues, separate is not equal. Female athletes consistently have to deal with fewer accolades, less press coverage and lower pay. A transgender sports league would undoubtedly be plagued with the same issues.

Beyond the trauma of sex-verification exams, these bills would cause further emotional damage to transgender youth. While we haven't seen an epidemic of transgender girls dominating sports leagues, we have seen high rates of anxiety, depression and suicide attempts. Research highlights that a major driver of these mental health problems is rejection of someone's gender identity. Forcing trans youth to play on sports teams that don't match their identity will worsen these disparities. It's a classic form of transgender conversion therapy, a discredited practice of trying to force transgender people to be cisgender and gender-conforming.

Though this can be hard for cisgender people to understand, imagine someone told you that you were a different gender and then forced you to play on the sports team of that gender throughout all of your school years. You'd likely be miserable and confused.

144

As a child psychiatry fellow, I spend a lot of time with kids. They have many worries on their minds: bullying, sexual assault, divorcing parents, concerns they won't get into college. What they're not worried about is transgender girls playing on girls' sports teams.

Legislators need to work on the issues that truly impact young people and women's sports—lower pay to female athletes, less media coverage for women's sports and cultural environments that lead to high dropout rates for diverse athletes—instead of manufacturing problems and "solutions" that hurt the kids we are supposed to be protecting.

About the Author

Jack Turban is a fellow in child and adolescent psychiatry at the Stanford University School of Medicine, where he researches the mental health of transgender youth. His writing has appeared in the New York Times, *the* Washington Post, *the* Los Angeles Times, *and more.*

The Psychology of Taking a Knee

By Jeremy Adam Smith and Dacher Keltner

What does it mean to kneel? What emotions and beliefs does this action communicate? Does your culture or group membership affect how you see gestures like kneeling?

Those are some of the scientific questions raised when San Francisco 49ers quarterback Colin Kaepernick decided last year to kneel, instead of stand, for "The Star-Spangled Banner" before a preseason game. Teammate Eric Reid joined him. Their cause? Police violence against unarmed black people.

His knee unleashed a movement—and triggered a chain of events that culminated last week in the president of the United States calling a player who kneels a "son of a bitch." Over the following days, dozens of NFL players—including entire teams—"took the knee" before their games. In response, crowds booed.

To some, Kaepernick and the players who kneel with him are "unpatriotic," "ungrateful," "disrespectful," "degenerate," to quote just a few of the descriptions hurled their way. To others, Kaepernick's act—for which he may have paid dearly, as he is now unsigned—makes him a hero.

What's going on?

At first glance, research into emotion and nonverbal communication suggests that there is nothing threatening about kneeling. Instead, kneeling is almost always deployed as a sign of deference and respect. We once kneeled before kings and queens and altars; we kneel to ask someone to marry, or at least men did in the old days. We kneel to get down to a child's level; we kneel to beg.

While we can't know for sure, kneeling probably derives from a core principle in mammalian nonverbal behavior: make the body smaller and look up to show respect, esteem, and deference. This is seen, for example, in dogs and chimps, who reduce their height to show submissiveness. Kneeling can also be a posture of mourning and sadness. It makes the one who kneels more vulnerable. In some situations, kneeling can be seen as a request for protection—which is completely appropriate in Kaepernick's case, given the motive of his protest.

As sports protests go, taking the knee might not seem nearly as subversive or dangerous as thrusting a black-power fist into the air, as Tommie Smith and John Carlos did during their medal ceremony at the 1968 Summer Olympics in Mexico City. Researchers David Matsumoto and Jess Tracy show that even blind athletes from over 20 countries thrust their arms in the air in triumph after winning, which reveals the deep-seated urge to signal power with that body-expanding gesture. You can also find power in the fist. In the Darwinian sense, the fist is the antithesis of the affiliative, open hand, but when we combine a raised arm with a fist it becomes something more communicative—a rallying cry. It's a gesture that seeks to bring one group together while warning another away.

None of that should be too surprising. But there is an important point of similarity in the raised black-power fist—which makes bodies bigger—and the bended knee, which makes us smaller. Both Carlos and Smith bowed their heads in Mexico City, in a sign of respect and humility that accompanies their social signal of strength and triumph. That mix of messages makes the black-power salute one of the most famous, complex, effective nonverbal protests in our lifetimes—one that we can see echoed on today's football field.

Which returns us to the kneel. Kneeling is a sign of reverence, submissiveness, deference—and sometimes mourning and vulnerability. But with a single, graceful act, Kaepernick invested it with a double meaning. He didn't turn his back as the anthem was played, which would have been a true sign of disrespect. Nor did he rely on the now-conventionalized black-power fist.

Rather, he transformed a collective ritual—the playing of the national anthem—into something somber, a reminder of how far we still have to go to realize the high ideal of equal protection under the law that the flag represents. The athletes who followed him are showing reverence for the song and the flag, but they are simultaneously deviating from cultural norms at the moment their knees hit the grass.

By transforming this ritual, the players woke us up. Our amygdalae activate as soon as our brains spot deviations from routine, social norms, and in-group tendencies. We want to know what's happening and why. We need to know if the deviation poses a threat to us or our group. This may start to explain why so many Americans reacted with such fear and rage to a few athletes kneeling on the field in the midst of a national ritual.

But there's a lot more to it than that.

"Group membership affects interpretation of body language because groups develop norms and expectations around behavior, language, and life," says our UC Berkeley colleague Rodolfo Mendoza-Denton, an expert on intergroup communication. "Breaking these norms is used intentionally to signal disagreement with the norms, as well as to signal that one is not conforming. It sparks strong emotion and backlash precisely because of its symbolic meaning—a threat to the status quo."

It matters that most of the athletes are black and much of the audience is white, that the ancestors of one group were brought here as slaves and the ancestors of the other were their owners. That's why, when Pittsburgh Steelers stayed in the locker room as the anthem played, one Pennsylvania fire chief called their coach a "no good n*****" on Facebook, amplifying the racial themes of the debate. That's why Michigan's police director called them "degenerates."

When you mix power differences with intergroup dynamics, more factors come into play. Our lab has found that high-power people (say, the president or members of the numerical majority) are more likely to misinterpret nonverbal behavior. The experience of having power makes us less accurate in reading suffering on the faces of strangers and emotions in static photos of facial expressions. Powerful people are less able to take the perspective of others; they're quicker to confuse friendliness with flirtatiousness. This is the empathy deficit of people in power, one found in many kinds of studies.

Thus, we should not be surprised that many white people misread the meaning of "taking the knee" and fail to see the respect, concern, and even vulnerability inherent in kneeling. Of course, it is also the case that some white people may want to see black people terrorized by police and politically disenfranchised. Any effort by African Americans, no matter how deferential, to raise these issues will incite anger from those who benefit—emotionally or materially—from America's racial hierarchy.

But from a psychological perspective, that political elucidation still doesn't quite explain the specific inability of a majority of white football fans to interpret taking the knee according to universal human norms. And why would they take the misperception further, to actually see this humble posture as an act of aggression against America?

There is some evidence from Princeton's Susan Fiske and Penn State's Theresa Vescio that high-power people, in not attending carefully to others, are more likely to stereotype others, and more likely to miss individual nuances in behavior. This means that some white-majority football fans may be falling victim to the stereotype of African Americans—particularly large, well-muscled, pro football players—as violent and aggressive. In fact, as we've discussed, kneeling is actually the opposite of an aggressive signal.

What's the way forward from here? One of us (Dacher Keltner) has co-authored a paper with colleague Daniel Cordaro that examines the expression of 20 emotions across five cultures. We found that that while most outward emotional expressions are shared or partially shared, a quarter are not. It's in that non-shared space that intercultural conflict flares up—but that conflict can sometimes lead to cross-pollination, as people come to comprehend each other and synchronize their gestures.

Will Americans one day look back on Kaepernick's symbolic act as a moment when we started to understand each other just a little bit better? When many kinds of people were galvanized to work concretely on the problems of police brutality and racial bias in the criminal justice system, instead of discounting the concerns of African Americans?

Perhaps. Such a time seems very distant from where we are right now, as our society's leaders foster racial antagonism and people cannot seem to recognize the emotion and belief behind even the gentlest of gestures. Change happens, but it doesn't happen all by itself. Sometimes, you need to kneel to conquer.

About the Author

Jeremy Adam Smith is editor of Greater Good *magazine and author or co-editor of four books, including* The Compassionate Instinct *and* Are We Born Racist?

Professional Sports Leagues Need to Reduce Their Carbon Footprint

By Seth Wynes

North American sports leagues have at best an inconsistent track record on sustainability; while they all offer some mix of elementary school environmentalism (tree planting, recycling, and preventing food waste), most bask in luxury on board hyperpolluting private planes traveling across the world. This behavior sends a mixed message.

Emissions from air travel are the most difficult to reduce in professional sports. It's not like they can do what everyone else does, and videoconference. But reducing emissions is possible. I examined some of the changes that could be made for a research article in the journal *Environmental Science and Technology*. In 2020, the National Basketball Association, the National Hockey League, Major League Baseball and the National Football League adjusted their schedules to reduce the chance of players and staff catching COVID. I found that by doing this, they inadvertently slashed their carbon footprint from air travel by a collective 22 percent per game. Emissions went back up when they returned to normal schedules, but there are still lessons to be learned.

The National Basketball Association is about to break for the 2022 All-Star Game, marking the midway point of the season. While it is too late to change anything this year, the NBA is especially well positioned to make some commonsense improvements that would reduce its carbon footprint substantially.

For one, the league could adopt a schedule that looks more like what Major League Baseball does: fly somewhere, play several games, then fly somewhere else. This scheduling construct is why, despite playing twice as many games per year, baseball's emissions were half that of basketball's in 2018.

This would be the most effective change the league could make, even if it might be a shock for NBA fans used to seeing their teams in a different town every few days. But a softer version would still cut emissions. During the 2020 regular season, the NBA only played 10 percent of games against the same opponent in a back-to-back fashion. The National Hockey League played 42 percent of its games that way. Each one of those games resulted in fewer climate-polluting flights.

Another simple way to reduce emissions is to schedule more games between neighboring teams. In the NBA, teams are divided into the Western and an Eastern Conference, and teams within conferences play each more often. So schedules are already optimized more than in the NFL or MLB, though an ambitious league could always push things further. Imagine introducing regional rivalries: pairs of teams that are close by play each other many times each season. So the New York Knicks have more games against the Brooklyn Nets, and none of those games would require flying.

Other ways to cut carbon include dropping overseas exhibition games, shortening the regular season and flying in smaller aircraft (picture something closer to business class seating for players, instead of first class plus massage tables). Cutting the NBA season by 10 games would save over 5,000 tonnes, or metric tons, of carbon dioxide per year, which is equivalent to what 2,200 medium-size cars produce in a year. To make up for the lost revenue of those eliminated games, you could introduce a mid-season tournament, which wouldn't add that much to flight emissions so long as you pick a central location like Chicago or Oklahoma City.

These changes wouldn't just benefit the environment; reducing travel time for players could improve performance. In the case of shortened seasons or baseball-style series, players would save entire days that could be used for resting instead of travel. More local games avoid long flights and time zone changes that result in injuries and worse performance. For leagues like the NBA where stadium attendance is driven by superstars coming to town, cutting back on injuries is a big financial consideration.

So why didn't the leagues adopt these policies a long time ago? Partially because of ratings; the leagues prioritize popular teams playing on days and times when they will draw in large viewership. This means that a California team might be in Utah one day, but in New York the next for a big matchup when both the league and broadcasters know people will watch. When it comes to scheduling, even player health and performance have been treated like a bench unit. If you're an unlucky team in the NBA, you might be asked to play four games in five days, and each game could even be in a different time zone!

But it's not just about ratings; status quo bias also plays a role. For instance, Jeanie Buss, owner of the storied Los Angeles Lakers franchise, says she is unwilling to consider shortening the NBA season, since this would make it harder to compare statistical records across years.

Given the competing goals of owners, players and league officials, change will be hard. As the leagues figure this out, there is one last important contribution that sports franchises could make: cut a deal with airlines to purchase credits for sustainable aviation fuels (SAFs) for every flight. These are alternatives to normal jet fuel; they may be synthesized from carbon dioxide or derived from plants or used cooking oil, but either way they have smaller carbon footprints.

SAFs aren't perfect, and they're expensive, but they do reduce emissions and we need to scale up their production. A year's worth of NBA air travel would require about five million gallons of SAFs, which is similar in size to a six million gallon deal just signed by Amazon Air. For companies that care about their green credentials and have the money to spare, why not be a part of catalyzing the growth of a critical climate technology?

In October 2019, Lebron James, one of the most recognizable faces of the NBA, had to evacuate his home in California, fleeing wildfires supercharged by an overheated planet. Climate change already affects players. Their leagues should start thinking about big changes now, because as the climate crisis worsens, doing only the little things just isn't going to fly anymore.

About the Author

Seth Wynes is a postdoctoral researcher studying climate change mitigation at Concordia University.

GLOSSARY

aerodynamic The qualities, such as shape, that allow an object to move easily through the air.

binary Composed of two, often opposite, things.

biomechanist A person who studies the movements of living things.

cisgender Describes a person whose gender identity corresponds to their birth sex.

countercultural Having to do with a culture that has norms and values that differ significantly from those of the mainstream culture.

echelon A level or grade in an activity or organization.

empirical analysis Interpretation or study that is based on evidence.

inertia The property of an object by which it stays still or in motion unless it is acted upon by another force.

intersex A person born with sex organs or characteristics that are not typically male or female.

intrinsic Essential to the nature of a thing.

neurocognitive Having to do with the neural structures that enable thought.

racial demographic Data on the population of people according to racial categories.

rotational velocity The speed at which something rotates.

superelite Highly superior in ability or other qualities.

transgender A person whose gender identity is different from the gender usually associated with their birth sex.

FURTHER INFORMATION

Ackerman, Daniel. "Avoiding the 'Bobblehead Effect': Strength Training Could Help Soccer Players." *Scientific American*, June 29, 2018, https://www.scientificamerican.com/article /avoiding-the-bobblehead-effect-strength-training-could-help -soccer-players/.

Blau, Max. "How Conor McGregor's Weight Loss Ahead of His Big Fight May Harm His Body." *Scientific American*, August 25, 2017, https://www.scientificamerican.com/article/how -conor-mcgregors-weight-loss-ahead-of-his-big-fight-may-harm -his-body/.

Drew, Liam. "How Athletes Hit a Fastball." *Nature*, March 31, 2021, https://www.nature.com/articles/d41586-021-00816-3.

Fiscutean, Andrada. "Data Scientists Are Predicting Sports Injuries with an Algorithm." *Nature*, March 31, 2021, https://www.nature.com/articles/d41586-021-00814-5.

Sanderson, Katherine. "Why Sports Concussions Are Worse for Women." *Scientific American*, September 23, 2021, https:// www.scientificamerican.com/article/why-sports-concussions -are-worse-for-women/.

Williams, Mark A. "Does Practice Make Perfect?" *Psychology Today*, March 9, 2021, https://www.psychologytoday.com/us/blog/how -athletes-are-made/202103/does-practice-make-perfect.

Williams, Mark A. "How Plasticity and Adaptability Create Great Athletes." *Psychology Today*, February 17, 2021, https:// www.psychologytoday.com/us/blog/how-athletes-are -made/202102/how-plasticity-and-adaptability-create-great -athletes.

Williams, Mark A. "What Influences Elite Athleticism?" *Psychology Today*, January 12, 2021, https://www .psychologytoday.com/us/blog/how-athletes-are -made/202101/what-influences-elite-athleticism.

CITATIONS

1.1 The Making of an Olympian by Rachel Nuwer (July 1, 2016); 1.2 How Olympic Figure Skaters Break Records with Physics by Tanya Lewis (February 14, 2022); 1.3 Hormone Levels Are Being Used to Discriminate Against Female Athletes by Grace Huckins (February 1, 2021); 1.4 Elite Athletes' Gut Bacteria Give Rodent Runners a Boost by Emily Willingham (June 24, 2019); 1.5 Four Myths About Testosterone by Rebecca M. Jordan-Young and Katrina Karkazis (June 18, 2019); 1.6 Head Injury and Chronic Brain Damage: It's Complicated by Brian Levine and Carrie Esopenko (September 1, 2017); 1.7 Olympic Gold May Depend on the Brain's Reward Chemical by Robin Wylie (August 5, 2016); 1.8 Go Figure: Why Olympic Ice Skaters Don't Fall Flat on Their Faces by Yasemin Saplakoglu (February 9, 2018); 1.9 The Olympic Motto, Cellular Memories, and the Epigenetic Effects of Doping by E. Paul Zehr (February 12, 2018); 1.10 Are We Reaching the End of World Records? by Karl J. P. Smith (August 5, 2016); 2.1 Home Advantage Doesn't Require Crowds, COVID Pro Soccer Matches Show by Diana Kwon (March 31, 2021); 2.2 How Overtraining Can Trap Athletes by Sarah Tuff Dunn (July 1, 2016); 2.3 Sports Psychologists Extend Their Counseling to Athletes' Coaches and Families by Katherine Harmon (August 1, 2012); 2.4 The Not-So-Hot Hand by John Matson (February 1, 2012); 2.5 Elite Soccer Refs Have Eagle-Eye Ability for Spotting Foul Play by Catherine Caruso (November 7, 2016); 2.6 Coaching Can Make or Break an Olympic Athlete by Rachel Nuwer (August 5, 2016); 2.7 No One Wins Gold for Practicing the Most by Karl J. P. Smith (August 5, 2016); 3.1 Why Baseballs Are Flying in 2019 by Steve Mirsky (July 9, 2019); 3.2 Where There's a Wills There's a Way to Explain the Home Run Rise by Meredith Wills and Steve Mirsky (September 30, 2018); 3.3 Blade Runners: Do High-Tech Prostheses Give Runners an Unfair Advantage? by Larry Greenemeier (August 5, 2016); 3.4 How Paralympic Wheelchairs and Prostheses Are Optimized for Speed and Performance by Sophie Bushwick (August 31, 2021); 3.5 Can Science Solve the Mystery of "Deflategate"? by Sarah Lewin Frasier (January 29, 2015); 3.6 Building the Ultimate Ultimate Disc by Laura G. Shields (January 2, 2018); 3.7 The Secret to Human Speed by Dina Fine Maron (August 1, 2016); 4.1 The NFL's Racist "Race Norming" Is an Afterlife of Slavery by Tracie Canada and Chelsey R. Carter (July 8, 2021); 4.2 Why Americans Love Baseball and Brits Love Soccer...er... Football by David Papineau (April 27, 2017); 4.3 What Does Success Mean for Long-Suffering Sports Fans? An Identity Crisis, Say Researchers by Eric Simons (October 30, 2015); 4.4 The Surprising Problem of Too Much Talent by Cindi May (October 14, 2014); 4.5 To Win a Sports Bet, Don't Think Too Much by Cindi May (July 23, 2013); 4.6 So, You Want Your Toddler to Grow Up to Win a Gold Medal by David Z. Hambrick (February 23, 2018); 4.7 Sports Results Affect Voter Behavior by Karen Hopkin (July 7, 2010); 4.8 Taming the Madness of Crowds by Gary Stix (March 1, 2009); 4.9 Trans Girls Belong on Girls' Sports Teams by Jack Turban (March 16, 2021); 4.10 The Psychology of Taking a Knee by Jeremy Adam Smith and Dacher Keltner (September 29, 2017); 4.11 Professional Sports Leagues Need to Reduce Their Carbon Footprint by Seth Wynes (February 16, 2022)

Each author biography was accurate at the time the article was originally published.

INDEX